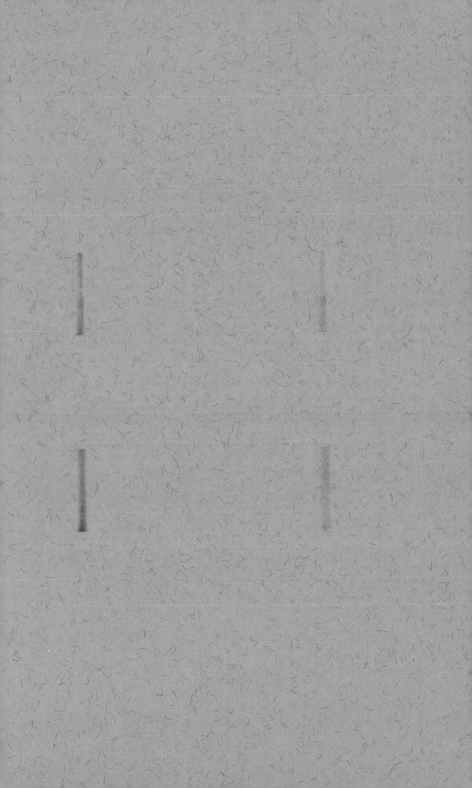

Threading the Currents

To Kris, Grant, and Marypat,
partners all

Threading
the Currents

A Paddler's Passion for Water

Alan S. Kesselheim

Illustrations by Marypat Zitzer

ISLAND PRESS / Shearwater Books
Washington, D.C. • Covelo, California

Some chapters in this book were previously published, in different form, in the following magazines. Reprint permission has been granted where necessary. "Thirst" appeared in *Backpacker,* May 1996; "Tempting the River Gods" appeared in *Canoe,* August 1990; "Consequences" appeared as "Trial by Water" in *Sports Afield,* September 1997; "Wintering Over" appeared as "Out in the Cold" in *Canoe,* December 1992; "Gravid Miles" appeared as "Am Pregnant, Will Paddle" in *Mothering,* Summer 1997; "Spring Dance on the Gallatin," "A Fly-Fishing Tradition," "Seeking the Wild," and "Taking the Yellowstone by Storm" appeared, in some cases with different titles, in *Big Sky Journal.*

Library of Congress Cataloging-in-Publication Data
Kesselheim, Alan S., 1952–
    Threading the currents : a paddler's passion for water / Alan S. Kesselheim.
      p.   cm.
    Includes bibliographical references and index.
    ISBN 1–55963–562–2. — ISBN 1–55963–563–0
    1. Kesselheim, Alan S., 1952– . 2. Canoeists—United States—Biography. 3. Canoes and Canoeing—North America. I. Title.
GV782.42.K47A3 1998
797.1'22'092—dc21   98-8076
[b]   CIP

Printed on recycled, acid-free paper

Manufactured in the United States of America
10 9 8 7 6 5 4 3 2 1

Acknowledgments   *ix*

Introduction   *xi*

Part I Headwaters

THIRST   3

TEMPTING THE RIVER GODS   10

CONSEQUENCES   17

COMING OF AGE   27

PARTNER   36

SOLO   45

Part II The Main Stem

REBOUNDING LAND   53

FINDING A WAY   63

SANDPIPER'S STORY   76

SOLITARY   86

THE BEAR   92

WINTERING OVER   102

RAIN   112

TIDES   120

A CHILD'S CRY   131

SUMMER OF BIRDS   135

THE ARMORED SEASON   146

ESKERS   153

BARREN LANDS   163

Part III Confluences

GRAVID MILES   171

BORDER FLOW   177

SPRING DANCE ON THE GALLATIN   190

A FLY-FISHING TRADITION   195

SEEKING THE WILD   202

FLOOD WATCH   207

TAKING THE YELLOWSTONE BY STORM   219

WIND   228

DISAPPEARING ACTS   237

Acknowledgments

THIS PROJECT IS AN expression of experiences that span more than half of my life. The great majority of the events described in this book were shared with companions, people who have had much to do with fueling the flame of my passion for water. Their comradeship has been a gift not always adequately recognized. Thanks to Craig Kesselheim, Beth Dilley, Kate Wilkinson, Dorcas Miller, Ursula Neese, Andrew and Sara Zitzer, Stephen Frick, Carolyn Hales, Sherry and Larry Eddy, and the other trip mates over the decades.

Writing is what I do for a living, but it is often a strange and aggravating business. My wife, Marypat, bears the brunt of the havoc wreaked on our family by virtue of my career choice and gets little of whatever glory comes along. Her support makes my writing possible. Jeanne Hanson is a literary agent with unflagging optimism and energy for the projects she takes on, including this one. I am grateful to the editors at Shearwater Books and Island Press, particularly Laurie Burnham, who saw promise in the early drafts and helped shepherd the manuscript through the grueling transformation into a book.

Introduction

THIS BUSINESS BEGINS with my father drinking out of a cow track on a dry Montana afternoon sometime around World War II. It ends with my three children lying naked on their bellies to drink out of a spring-fed creek not fifty miles from that same spot, as the raven flies. Full circle, near enough.

In between are the threads that run through a quarter century dominated by water. Threads that stitch together hunks of landscape as disparate as the canyons of the Rio Grande along the Mexican border and the glacially squashed rim of Hudson Bay. Threads that knit some kind of loose pattern out of decades of immersions into wild places, interactions between people in the midst of blank gaps on the map, intersections with wildlife, and elemental confrontations with tide and wind and rain and ice.

Years ago, when I started to write this, my thought was to pinpoint the most vivid moments in several decades of being on and around water. These snapshots of experience, I thought, would crystallize the essence of my passion for the places water takes me, a passion I don't always completely fathom. As much as anything, it was an attempt to understand what lies behind my obsession.

I still think that. But as the work unfolded, I realized that something else was happening, something more profound and encompassing than the retelling of sharp and evocative moments. It came clear that what I was dealing with was only superficially about water, my time traveling in wilderness, and the events that occurred along the way.

I saw that water was only the medium I chose and that paddling in a boat was simply the technique and the vehicle. As I began to pick up and follow these threads of current that run, seemingly unconnected, back through the decades, patterns began to sharpen and themes began to resonate.

What came looming up as I wound my way in deeper was the stripped-down, unadulterated marrow of life. Elemental joys. Death. Love. Revelation. Comedy. Friendship. Birth. Forgiveness. Trust. Patience. Humility. Miracle. Fear. Endurance. Anger. Epiphanies of the spirit. The big stuff.

This was not about being in boats and paddling stretches of water any more than music is only people with instruments in front of sheets full of scribbling, or any more than mountaineering is nothing but the coupling of rumpled quadrants of the planet and climbers with racks of hardware.

The liquid element and these travels were my way of latching on to the most compelling and important facets of life, and the very act of embarking on these journeys took me, by definition and despite any intention to the contrary, to the heart of things. In the watery wilds I am the most alive, the most clear headed and unburdened. I am at my best, in spite of myself.

The order of things, an order that grows incrementally murky and conflicted in the workaday confusion, shuffles into a kind of simple clarity. On the water the stuff that seems so terribly important at home falls away into the obscurity it deserves, and I am left almost free. I live as directly as I am capable of, listening to the winds and currents, communicating with other species, being with my partners, and feeling my way toward a sense of place, out there in the moment.

I make it sound as purposeful and disciplined, and perhaps as self-conscious, as a religious quest, but I had no idea this would happen. It snuck up on me.

Although I grew up in an adventurous outdoor family, paddling was never a very prominent feature of our activities. Family outings in boats, often as not, had wet and humiliating endings. Attending a canoe camp during a summer in junior high was the most serious introduction I had to water travel.

After college I took over stewardship of the venerable family canoe, a seventeen-foot, dinged-up aluminum lake boat with the nickname *Pebble-Banger*, during a stint when my parents lived overseas. I carried on the legacy of mishap and ignobility that was the fate of that canoe as I learned the rudiments of paddling technique and penetrated the frontiers of bad judgment on the water.

Then my brother invited me on a canoe trip into the wilds of Quebec. That journey very nearly ended in tragedy less than a week in. It was the trip during which I lost my innocence about wilderness. But it also ignited my lust for the dynamic power of water and for the wild potential it can unleash. Since that trip, twenty years ago, I haven't gone nine months without being on the water in some sort of boat.

In that time I have paddled thousands of miles in a variety of craft, all over North America. The ways of water have slowly etched themselves across the geography of my psyche. I don't so much understand them as feel them. The way, for instance, a slab of river will wheel around the deep corner on a bend. How current going through a field of rocks is separated into filaments, distinct as braids of hair. Or the eerie way shafts of sunlight will stab through truly deep lake water on a calm day. When I look at a map now, I am pulled in by the blue bloodlines that gather it together— places I have been, watery pulses I have felt, and spots I want, still, to go.

I have kept on, in large measure, because I have been graced with a series of paddling partners who have fallen prey to the same passion and who have embraced my company. Paddling with a partner is very much like dancing together. You move in concert to the rhythms of current and wave, harmonize your interactions, react to each other's moves, sense each other's intentions a beat ahead, read the water notes in the tension of body language. You come to know your partner's best and worst moves. And, when you step on each other's toes, you generally get wet.

My most long-standing companion is the woman I married, Marypat. We are linked together to house and children and land and seventeen years of shared history. Other than our children, the thing that binds us to each other most is the miles of water we have crossed in boats. Our time on water is the thing that we hold sacred, separate and distinct from everything else. The thing that is unequivocally ours. Twice we have paddled away from civilization together and not come back for fourteen months. When I think about our commitment to each other, our most fundamental connection, it is the currents of the continent that weave through it all, vital as sinew and muscle.

What appeared, when I started out on this writing journey, to be a collection of unconnected pieces, loosely organized on a liquid theme, slowly stitched itself into some kind of sense, all of a piece. Although the span of time crosses a quarter of a century and the geography reaches from the Chihuahuan Desert to the Arctic Ocean, the threads that start out like the first, tiny, far-flung trickles of a watershed come inexorably toward each other and join up like the filaments of current jostling down the main stem of a big river.

That it came full circle was another surprise. What is reassuring about circles is that there is no end to them. When you close one up, you are only poised at a new beginning.

Part I

Headwaters

Thirst

STRANGE, the things that hang up, year after year, in the filter of memory. It's been a quarter century since my father told me the story about drinking out of a cow track. Of all the things I once knew, should know, would like to know about my dad, it's the image of him puckered up over a muddy pool set in the round, embedded track of a cow that hangs in there through the decades.

But then, it stuck in his mind, too, because it had to have been twenty-five years after the event when he told me.

Fifty years ago, more or less, August, and he was a teenager hiking in the low, dry mountains near Nye, Montana. He'd been alone all day. Hiking, back then, was not the fad it is now. It was late afternoon, the sun was plenty high in the sky, and he'd been out of water since before lunch.

Somewhere in the messy inheritance of what my parents have given me, there in the clutter of genes and mannerisms and pitfalls of habit, is my father's tendency to eschew the mainstream for what beckoned to him. He jogged on the dirt ranch roads a generation before anyone had heard of Lycra. He was one of the first conscientious objectors in Montana's history. And he headed off, often as not alone, and as often as possible, into the hills.

On that dry afternoon, my father sucked on pebbles, worked up a little spit. The intermittent stream he'd counted on turned out to be a dry ditch full of the arid clatter of grasshopper wings. His feet hurt, heat shimmered off the exposed trail. There was no shade anywhere, and there were miles to go.

He thought about other things—the girls at school in Billings, basketball, the old taxicab his brother had just bought. But he was thirsty. Before long his mind ran off toward images of pitchers full of ice water, juicy oranges, the sound of the creek behind the ranch house, the way a cube of ice would feel in his mouth, melting there, burning with cold.

In this dumb, parched mental haze he tromped past a fat cow track full of liquid. He stopped, went back, and looked down at the turbid puddle, sunlight glinting up off its surface.

"I didn't even think much," he told me. "I just got down and drank it."

It is a singular image. My father, a lean young man down on his knees, bent over as if he were kissing the dry trail. Only he was kissing what he fervently hoped was water, sucking the warm, muddy puddle dry.

"It was incredibly refreshing," he said. "It got me home."

In the body of a 145-pound human being, about what my father weighed back then, there are forty-two quarts of water. Typically, more than two-thirds of it resides inside cells and the remaining third refreshes other corporeal spaces. Ten and one-half gallons of water, more than half my father's body weight.

Not surprisingly, given the extent to which we are liquid creatures, thirst is ranked as a primary human motivation, alongside hunger, sex, and the avoidance of pain. Until we are thirsty, it rarely crosses our minds; once we are, it is all we can think about.

Water oozes out of us in a quiet, constant seep, escaping like a slow-drip spring. We breathe it out, make fog with it on cold days. It flushes away in our urine. Even when we aren't exercising, we perspire constantly. Sitting still, we shed two and one-half percent of our body's water every day. If we don't drink, we'll lose two to three pounds daily in water alone, a decidedly unwholesome weight loss plan. We can do without food of any consequence for weeks on end, but water holds us on a far shorter leash.

Add searing heat to the equation, along with some strenuous exercise, and water positively cascades out of us. In extreme cases, dehydration can accelerate to shock and death in a matter of hours.

The niggling voices of concern start faintly, after a few hours without fluids, somewhere back in the dark recesses of the brain. My father probably heard that early whisper of alarm shortly after his lunch. Osmoreceptor cells in the hypothalamus, at the base of the brain, are responsible for those first worrisome murmurs. They are responding to a slight fluid loss in the cells.

"We're thirsty," they say.

We ignore them, tell them to be patient; walk faster and think about other primary human motivations.

My dad's mouth gets dry and chalky. His tongue starts to feel like a thick cotton rag. Saliva is scarce. Swallowing, because there's nothing to lubricate his throat, becomes painful. He stoops to pick up a pebble, rolls it against his jeans to get the dirt off, and pops it into his mouth. The rest of his human motivations pale in the face of this gnawing obsession, this liquid craving. The pebble, at first a novelty, something to focus on, becomes increasingly unsatisfactory, more and more like a lump of grit.

Receptor cells in the digestive tract join the chorus. The heart, kidneys, pituitary gland, and vagus nerve respond in alarm. Water diffuses back and forth across cell membranes in a struggle to maintain equilibrium in the face of decreasing volume. Blood turns slightly more viscous and sluggish, harder for the heart to push.

Right about then my father sees the shimmering cow track. As he said, he didn't have to think about it much.

Only once have I been that thirsty. I was in the Grand Canyon, one of several instructors leading a group of criminal offenders on a course designed to prepare them for the transition to life outside the penitentiary. Taking hoods to the woods, we called our work. A certain level of physical and emotional stress was part of the agenda. Dying of thirst was not.

Winter days in the depths of the Grand Canyon of the Colorado can be as hot and dry as summer days in Montana. We were hiking a faint, little-used trail along a shale rim below the Tonto Bench, still well above the river. Our destination for the day was a riverside beach, but things kept delaying us. Someone's blister needed attention. A pack strap broke. A prickly pear thorn worked through a boot and had to be tugged out.

Burro trails led us astray again and again, petering out into crumbly shards of red and green rock full of dusty, unblinking lizards. Half a dozen times we had to drop packs and scout for the path. The men guzzled their water. When we lost the trail for good, we were already rationing the last quart, and by the time we found our way down the steep side of a tributary canyon that we hoped would take us to the river, it was dusk and the water had been gone for hours.

Even so, it was only a mile to the river, a straight shot down the dry, sandy wash. Maybe we would find a pool along the way. We slogged through the deep sand, thoughts full of the liquid ribbon ahead, right up to the abrupt lip of a dry waterfall, a desert pour-off. Then we stood there in the gathering twilight, heads bowed as if in prayer, looking over the edge. It was a short drop, just ten or twelve feet. In wet times it would be a loud cascade. We all considered that waterfall, and the Colorado River beyond, with throat-catching vividness.

While the group prepared a dry camp, Kris and I took a string of water bottles and bellied over the edge. Kris was a strong, big-boned woman with a hundred-watt smile and a quick wit. She could hold her own in rapid-fire street Spanish with men two days out of the pen and render sullen, knife-happy delinquents into sheepish kids desperate for her attention. Between stints leading wilderness courses, she and I lived together in a one-bedroom adobe apartment on the fringe of a barrio in Santa Fe.

The small canyon twisted down through dark, riven volcanic rock. Night slipped over us with the weight of a yoke. The empty bottles clattered thinly against one another. A quarter mile farther on, another pour-off confronted us, maybe twenty feet long. We scrambled down a series of ledges, the interior clamor for liquid relief subduing any qualms about our ability to climb back up.

Then, almost immediately, we were brought up short by a falls of indeterminate length, a dark, sheer gully corkscrewing out of sight through the ancient brown bedrock. We peered down along the wan beam of our flashlight. It is a mark of our thirst that we both stood there, silent for a long minute, considering a way down.

When the group of men—men who were usually taciturn,

some sullen, and without exception careful with their emotions—heard us returning, they broke into boyish yells of triumph. We could see their shapes perched above us on the brink of the little dry falls.

"Water! Water!" they cried, turning clumsy jigs in the sand.

I'd have given a lot to hand cool, sweaty bottles full of Colorado River up from the darkness.

"No water," I said instead, and the canyon's silence washed back in. The men turned away and shuffled back to their packs.

All night I heard people turning in their bags, moaning out loud when they fell asleep. In the moments when I was free of insistent thoughts, when I fell into a light sleep, I hallucinated more than I dreamed, in tortured outbursts from a thirsty being who should consist of two-thirds water but was drying out fast.

Kris and I rose before dawn. We had talked over our options well into the night and had settled on a plan to climb to a higher ledge, skirt the sheer section of canyon, and then try to find a way down. We might even reconnect with the trail, which had to be somewhere close by.

Cold sat in the canyon depths like fog. I saw goose bumps on Kris's legs, but it would be hot soon enough. I kept swallowing, trying to lubricate my throat, but the saliva was foam, not water. We looked back at the men, curled up in sleeping bags on the rocky valley floor. Then we started climbing steeply through the loose talus. I kept tamping down the dead-end thoughts, turning away from the seduction of panic.

A desert bighorn showed itself in silhouette at a jagged gap of rock and then melted away. I tried to breathe through my nose to ease the rawness in my throat. We moved slowly but urgently, minds busy with contingency plans; busy, too, with images of fitful men huddled in the sand.

Then we stumbled over a rock cairn. Our faint path. In less than half an hour, the day still dim gray, we were at the Colorado.

I draped myself over a boulder and filled a quart water bottle with the cloudy green river. River that had run through Grand Junction and Glenwood Springs, through fertilized field and cow pasture, river that had been squeezed through turbines and had unguessable effluents poured into it. I put the bottle to my mouth and drank down the whole gritty quart.

Just then, with the cold water soaking the dry spaces in my body, seeping through cell membranes, thinning my blood, drowning the general alarm, I thought of my father, prostrate in front of a wet cow track in the dust of an August Montana afternoon, half a century earlier.

Tempting the River Gods

Outings with Kris had a way of gravitating to the unpredictable extremes, either life threatening, as in running out of water in the Grand Canyon, or outrageous and bizarre, as with the canoe trip that ended with me standing on a boulder in the middle of the Rio Grande wearing nothing but a visor and a pair of weathered tennis shoes.

The setting is idyllic. Fall in northern New Mexico—desert-toned landscape under a dome of seamless blue, cottonwood trees rustling with yellow leaves; warmth that rekindles memories of summer but without the searing heat. A reminder that we've already slipped into accepting the inevitable coming of winter, a subtle slide toward attitudinal hibernation. A day to be out in.

It is one of the rare weekends when Kris and I get to share time. The curse of working as outdoor instructors in the same program is that we are often saddled with alternating rotations. Even though we live together, some months we see each other only on a handful of days.

Kris suggests a jaunt down the Rio Grande in the dented Grumman lake canoe I have borrowed from my parents while they are out of the country. Any other waterway within striking distance of Santa Fe is too low by October to be much fun. By autumn the rivers are ebbing toward their quiet winter pace; the Rio Grande is rippling through the canyons it charges down during the melt season, relaxed as a Sunday drive.

We pack up a lunch, and an hour later we have launched the canoe. Mostly we float along. A few families have responded to the fall day by driving down to the river to fish or picnic. We exchange greetings. Only minor fast water punctuates the steady tug of current; we proceed at a sedate pace into the deepening canyon. Basalt cliffs begin to rise higher above the river, constricting our view. Fewer roads penetrate as we approach the boundary of Bandelier National Monument. We are alone.

Once in a while we practice an eddy turn or another maneuver, but it feels good just to cruise, to watch the landscape. Ravens croak overhead, their outstretched shadows diving across the brown cliffs. A few rapids challenge us, but at this water level we handle them easily.

We pull over above the one formidable bit of whitewater along the run in order to scout it from shore. At higher water the constriction rapid is a fast, big-volume chute with huge waves. Even at this moderate level I feel the familiar tightening knot of anxiety and excitement. The canoe is by no means designed for whitewater, and I am still in the early part of the paddling learning curve. As a team our canoeing skills are only adequate. Across the river I can barely make out the aluminum glint of a submerged canoe pinned under a rock by the full brunt of current, a shiny warning against complacency.

We discuss strategy, focusing on the loud water before

us, and forget the spell of the day in the tension. Then, with life vests on, we are back in the boat, setting up, kneeling for stability. The river sucks us along more and more irresistibly. The waves are big enough to give us a rollicking ride. The canoe twists and plunges, taking some water over the bow. I feel an inch of cold river sloshing around my knees, but we are right where we want to be, our strokes solid and tight. I glimpse the battered underwater casualty again as we sweep past on the back of the river, and we're through.

It seems a good time to have lunch. A sunny sandbar offers itself. Content in the knowledge that we've passed the tricky part of the river, we soak up warmth and readjust ourselves to the desert surroundings. It gets hot, so Kris and I strip down for a dip in the cold, silty water and then let our skin dry under the friendly sun. When we get back in the canoe, we don't bother to put our clothes on but just toss them loosely into the bottom. It's that kind of day.

At the mouth of Frijoles Canyon, inside Bandelier National Monument, a final boulder-strewn riffle precedes the lengthy flatwater paddle that a downstream dam has inflicted on canoeists. The water level is much different from what it was the only other time I've run the rapid, a year earlier. That time I was with a group in a raft, but I remember the spot well.

"You think we should scout?" Kris calls back from the bow. I stand up, looking for the route I remember, and identify what appears to be a clean line. I resist going to shore again so soon.

"I think we're okay," I say. "Let's head for that top 'V.'"

But as we approach, I see things I couldn't see from upstream. What I thought was a clean shot is littered with hidden obstacles. Instead of taking us through, the "V" actually feeds right into a rocky barrier. We should have scouted. By the time I see our error, it's too late to get to shore.

"Let's ferry left!" I shout, knowing it's not going to work. The ferry angle goes wrong. We're more broadside than we should be. The whitewater has us; the boulders loom close and large. Kris yells something that I don't hear. The boat is almost fully broadside, and our paddling harmony is gone.

Then, the shock of cold, green water. I hear myself sputtering. The boat is in front of me, gaping into the current, filling with river. Kris has disappeared. I flail toward the near end of the canoe, but as I reach it I, hear the dull thunk of hull against rock and the boat shudders to a stop, pinned across two boulders, a sickening crease in its hull. As the current adapts to the new obstacle in its path, the canoe fills with piles of water and settles.

I scramble to the top of a rounded volcanic rock and look anxiously downstream for Kris. She is only ten feet away, clinging to a tree root wedged down by the current. Her face has the universal expression worn by victims of natural calamity—astonishment, shock, personal affront.

"You okay?" I ask.

She nods. "I got sucked right under the boat." She begins hauling herself against the current toward her own midriver island of basalt.

My attention turns to the foundered boat. Damage has been done. I can tell that some of the rivets have popped out. An oblique crease dents the boat toward the stern, but by being pinned across two rocks the canoe has avoided being folded in two.

I am still berating myself for being too lazy and confident to stop and look at the run. The rapid is embarrassingly minor. With a brief scout we could have shot through and been a mile downstream by now. Gingerly I work my way back into the river next to our craft and find that I can actually stand upstream of it to get leverage on the hull.

Initially it doesn't even occur to me that I might not be able to free the boat. But as I test different angles, even get my whole body underwater and heave up mightily, I begin to appreciate the power of the river. The canoe is immovable; it doesn't even wiggle.

Kris has made her way to the other rock the boat is lodged against. For twenty minutes or more we struggle against the current. Then, each standing on our tiny island, we appraise each other. Kris is wearing running shoes and a cap, nothing else. I sport tennis shoes and a visor. The rest is sunburned flesh. We chuckle at each other and then laugh out loud for a bit.

The humor doesn't last long because now we're going to have to walk two miles on a well-used trail to the park headquarters and then hitchhike to our car. I can tell that Kris is pondering the same conclusion. We laugh a little more, but now it's nervous laughter. I kneel over the boat and search through the roiling river water for bits of clothing. Nothing. The river has washed them away.

I imagine various all-too-possible vignettes—meeting young families along the trail; arriving at the busy parking lot; explaining to a receptionist at the visitor center why I need a towel; standing on the highway, offering our thumbs, and everything else, to passing recreational vehicles.

"Hey!" Kris interrupts my morose thoughts. "What about that stuff sack with my running clothes? Didn't we tie that to the seat?"

She's leaning out over the boat as she talks, feeling back to the stern seat. The current is strongest there, but she finds the string and the bag, bouncing and tugging in the river.

"Careful! Don't lose that stuff!" I walk across on the hull

of the canoe to help. It takes a full ten minutes to unhitch the knot, but then we hold the precious bag of garments, scanty as it is.

Kris peers inside and then pulls out the wet contents— one pair women's size medium running shorts and one women's size medium stretch leotard. I ponder momentarily how to wear the stuff sack, but the applications elude me.

Kris looks at me and then looks back at the clothes. "I guess I get the leotard, you get the shorts." We laugh again nervously.

I'm not a small man. Running shorts are diaphanous things, made to economize on weight and wind drag. Even though I'm quite motivated, it's a struggle to wiggle into Kris's shorts. The coverage about equals that of a small bandana, and I am uncomfortably reminded of junior-high locker room pranks we called wedgies. Kris, in her skin tight, sleeveless leotard, looks oddly attired for hiking, but not nearly so outlandish as me. I decide to carry one of our paddles along as sort of an explanatory prop for the hikers we might meet.

We hop to shore across a string of rocks and start off, shoes squelching water, my gait visibly affected by the constricting garb. Now and again I hear Kris giggling softly behind me. I make menacing gestures with the paddle, which only goad her into hysterical laughter, so I ignore her.

Within a quarter mile the shorts are uncomfortable enough that I'm thinking about splitting them apart at the seam. That may happen anyway. About then the first hikers come upon us, a couple with two young children. The adults choose feigned nonchalance and an inner-city aversion of eyes. The kids gape. I mutter something that is supposed to be construed as a greeting.

Soon we start encountering lots of people. We grow

brazen and callous to our effect and stride past them, making no attempt to communicate; I use the paddle as a hiking staff. At least Kris isn't laughing anymore. Between groups of hikers I try to pluck the shorts out of my crotch.

Finally, we arrive at the busy parking lot. We shortcut to the exit road and start hitching. Kris is clearly the more presentable envoy, so she stands in front. I half hide behind her and extend my bare arm toward the roadway, wearing a benign expression, as if hitchhiking in a loincloth is normal weekend fare. A great many vehicles pass by, seeming to accelerate as they do. They are mostly station wagons, campers, and motor homes. Children turn around in their seats to gawk. Adults pretend we're invisible.

It's remarkable that anyone would stop and more remarkable still that the car that eventually does is a Mercedes-Benz driven by an older couple. They politely refrain from inquiry as we settle into the plush rear seat. Thinking the canoe paddle a little scruffy for the interior, I leave the window rolled down and hold it outside as we drive through Los Alamos toward our vehicle.

It is a quiet ride. In less than half an hour we're back to the car. We retrieve the keys we hid under the bumper and are on our way home. It isn't until we're halfway to Santa Fe that we discuss strategy.

"You know," Kris begins, "I don't think anyone knew we went paddling today."

Another mile slips by. "Maybe we could get some rope and carabiners and go back tomorrow. We could have the canoe sitting in the yard before anyone knows the difference."

Consequences

I̶T'S A SUNNY DAY in northern Quebec, sleepy with July warmth and slightly breezy. We've been dawdling down a tea-colored stream near the moss-deep divide between water that flows north to Hudson Bay and water that pours south across glacier-tempered rock to the Gulf of St. Lawrence. The stream connects two lakes, one with a crescent beach we camped on the night before and the other a north–south taper slashing through twenty miles of rockbound, spruce-stubbled fastness.

As we float along, we fish. Craig hooks a northern pike that he says feels, at first, like a waterlogged branch. It thrashes water only as it's hauled from the tannic liquid world and into the sun-washed air. There it lies, lifeless as a piece of stove-length firewood, in the bottom of their canoe; plenty for dinner.

Kris and I have leapt across the continent from New Mexico to join my brother and his partner for this expedition. We have been together for two years, but at the end of this trip I will be taking a teaching job at a small college in

Wisconsin and Kris will be going to graduate school in California. Our first journey into the boreal wilds is also the watershed in our relationship. We pay lip service to a future with possibilities, but we both know that this is it.

Four days in. Two yellow canoes. The iron-dark, big-muscled Moisie River is coming up soon, only a day or two south. Until now the river has been a theoretical journey on maps down a snaking blue ribbon in a land full of ribbons, a southward meander crossing brown contour lines like stair steps, broken up by such a density of crosshatches that the cartographers resorted to space-saving R's and F's rather than writing out "Rapids" and "Falls." Even now, still dozens of miles distant, I listen for the river in winds from the south, in just the way I might wake late at night to a train whistle and strain for the last, far moan of the freight as it picks up speed leaving town. I lean toward the Moisie's sound, its pull, the funnel of frothy, dangerous velocity that will suck us south all the way to the ocean-swelled St. Lawrence.

It is still sunny when we break out along the shore of Opacopa Lake through a stream-wide gap in the woods. We rest there a minute, adjusting to the horizon, assessing the broad bulb of water, feeling the unhindered breeze.

A decision. Should we cross a mile-wide bay to save distance or hug the shoreline and stay safe? It is a decision like any of a dozen made each day: do we angle into waves or hit them straight, steer left or right of a midriver rock, sneak along the edge of a rapid or portage, wait out a rain or pull on our gear and keep paddling? Each one can mean life or death. At the same time, each is as mundane as crossing a street.

The wind is blowing across the lake, broadside to our route. There are waves but few whitecaps. It looks as if the crossing would save us at least a mile, and the far point is a sharp line of spruce trees, tangible and within reach. We shrug into life vests, kneel on the bottom, and start paddling out.

The cadence changes. It is lake rhythm, wind and wave and deepwater music. The canoe rolls beneath us in time. Our knees shift, hips swing, and paddles hit in a rough beat. From the stern I watch the lift and drop of waves, adjusting to the larger ones. Some slap up the side of the boat right to the gunwale, but we don't take on water. The far point doesn't seem as close now. The waves are bigger than we thought. Craig and Susan are just ahead, their boat climbing and diving, paddles flashing.

I strike a balance between heading straight across and facing into the wind so that I slice waves at a slight angle and the wind pushes the hull sideways like a ferry in river current. There are whitecaps now, blinking around us like flashes of liquid lightning.

It seems a long time, with wind snatching at my clothes and the heavy boat riding far from shore. But we are halfway. I can distinguish the larger boulders on the point, the ice-racked line of moss and dirt behind them. We still haven't shipped any water, and the lake music is a tune we are dancing to, a little grimly, but dancing still.

When I glance up, I see that Craig and Susan have gone over. Their canoe is a dull yellow log with waves breaking over it, and the two of them are flailing nearby.

"Shit, they're over!"

Kris and I have both stopped paddling. The waves heave under our rudderless weight. A small splash, the first, breaks over the gunwale, and we start up again. I think that if I blink, the picture will change and order will be restored.

In a minute we are up to them. The capsized canoe is dead in the water. We bump against it and circle around, forced to backpaddle to hold our place. The wind shoves at us and the boat bucks in the waves. Craig and Susan are the more experienced paddling team by far; they have guided trips in the Far North. Kris and I are the neophytes, and this is our first real expedition to the northern wilds. It should be us in the water. I fight off the certainty that we will join them, that it is only a matter of time and the right wave.

Craig is swimming toward us, towing a waterlogged pack. "I don't know how long the packs will float," he says between breaths. "If we lose this stuff, we're in trouble."

I am looking at my brother's face in the cold, weltered water. The picture is all wrong. He is pale with the shock but oddly matter-of-fact, surprisingly composed. "What happened?" I ask.

"A rogue wave." He has one hand on our gunwale now and looks up at me soberly. We're having an analytical conversation. "We must have leaned wrong. The downslope gunwale caught in the water, and we were over."

He muscles the pack a bit out of the water and I catch a corner of canvas. "Careful!" Kris warns, as I strain and Craig kicks under the weight. The pack streams water and slaps heavily into our boat. We have to paddle constantly, circling the stranded canoe and our two comrades. Susan is herding another pack toward us through the water.

"We can't tip," Kris says, her voice strident with fear. She is saying what everyone knows. If she and I go over, we will all die together in the frigid lake.

The second pack is heavier yet, more full of water. It takes both Craig and Susan pushing from underneath, me tugging hard, and Kris bracing with her paddle off the far side to lever it over the gunwale. It rides on top of our own load, leaking water into the canoe and raising our center of gravity. We are so deep in the water now that every wave slurps past the brink of the gunwales.

Craig is busy with the equipment pack, the heaviest one by far, full of frying pan and ax and tarp and blocks of cheese. We can't even get it a foot out of the water. "It'll sink us!" I am shouting into my brother's face, as if the wind has become monumentally loud, our struggle deafening. "Tie it to the stern line!"

"We have to get this stuff to shore." I am desperately working to keep our stern to the waves. "We'll unload and get back as quick as we can. You guys stay with the canoe. Haul yourselves as much out of the water as possible; conserve your strength."

The two of them stroke slowly toward their foundered boat. I have to quell the edge of panic that makes me want to flail at the water with my paddle. Pace yourself, pace yourself, I keep muttering, but within minutes I am huffing for air. The canoe is an absolute leaden pig. A pool several inches deep sloshes around my knees; once in a while a passing wave pours in a little more. The equipment pack is a two-hundred-pound anchor pulling the stern down.

I pick out a boulder onshore. We paddle till our arms ache and still the rock hasn't moved. It is taking too long. The two of us say nothing. Every so often I crane my neck for a glance back. Sometimes I see Craig and Susan, two dots of life-vest color draped across the yellow log. Sometimes they are out of sight in a wave trough, the lake a heart-stopping emptiness.

We've made a terrible mistake. We should have taken people first. They are dying in the water while we inch toward land. We could have tied off the packs somehow and come back for them later; so what if we lost some things. When Craig came over with the first pack, with that practical certainty on his face, it never occurred to me that if we took packs on board we would have to leave people behind for a second trip. Then, once we'd gotten the packs in, it was as if we couldn't undo our strategy, had to play it out.

It isn't at all certain that we will make it, either. Water is coming in regularly, sinking us deeper. My arms are numb with fatigue. The fatalistic shadow of defeat looms in my thoughts like an eclipse. How long has it been? Kris has her head down and is paddling mechanically. Maybe it's too demoralizing for her to watch the shore. Maybe she is making the same assessment I am.

Suddenly I can see the sandy bottom. The water is still over my head, but soon the equipment pack will be dragging. Riveted by the sight, I mutter incantations against the chance that it is only a sandbar and that the bottom will drop away again. It doesn't. I can feel the equipment pack bump and catch.

Without saying a thing, I vault over the side. Kris jerks around in alarm and sees me chest deep in the waves. But with me pushing the boat while Kris paddles, we go much faster. Closer in, Kris jumps out, too, and we haul together into the surf breaking against round boulders.

There is no time for talk and no energy for it anyway. We throw the packs a few yards up the shore, just out of the waves' reach, tip the boat over to empty it of water, and turn it back into the waves. I have to overcome a visceral moment that I am ashamed of: the impulse, now that we have found land, to stay there, to survive. But I see those distant dots of color rise and fall in the wild lake as we take the first strokes into the implacable wind.

The boat is light now, buoyant, almost dangerously so. With the packs, even if we rode low, we were solid and steady in the water. Now the wind shoves us around; there are precarious moments. Still, compared with the trip in, and despite the strong wind, we make good headway.

The exertion of getting to shore and the overwhelming urgency to return for our partners have been so consuming that I haven't given a thought to how we'll execute the rescue, what aid we might need to administer. It is enough to do this simple task—get to shore and come back, quickly. It is enough, for now, to aim the bow for the two of them out there. I wonder if they see us coming, if they are talking, or if, like us, they are conserving strength and realizing that there isn't much worth saying.

The world has focused down to this tableau, this small bay on a remote northern lake that has been free of ice for less than a month. This wind-lashed sunny afternoon with four people, two canoes, and things gone irrevocably wrong. There is nothing else—no wider world, no families, no plans, none of the passions that seemed, minutes ago, to drive our lives. Only the next wave, the target of color, the screaming wind, our labored breathing.

When we finally get close, I see Craig's head up, watching our approach. It is as if we are seeing each other again after an extended separation, as if, say, we'd spent an isolated winter apart and, at this first meeting of spring, we need to take each other's measure again.

"We're in bad shape," he says, and he sounds as if he's just downed a pint of Jack Daniels. Susan barely lifts her head. They are dying right now, the cold lake sapping their life, chilling their blood, drugging them.

"Can you bring Susan to the side of our boat?" I ask him.

He starts to move, almost languidly, toward her. They have been lovers, but their romance is over. The recent months have been a bitter and painful trial. That relationship is over, and they have come on this trip out of loyalty to the adventure and commitment to us, not to be together. But if we can't do this next thing, they will die with each other.

The activity seems to rouse Craig. He pulls Susan off the boat, embracing her, he swims toward us. She manages to kick feebly. He latches her white fingers over our gunwale.

"Craig!" I am trying to haul him up from the cold depths with my voice. "Get around the canoe to the other side. Steady us when we pull her in.

"Susan! You have to help us." She nods, but it is dreamlike, and I feel as if I'm shouting across a great distance to someone who's walking away.

"Try to keep our bow into the waves," I say to Kris. We are both kneeling, hunkered as low in the boat as we can get. She looks back and I fix on her brown eyes. They are saying that we, too, will be dying if this doesn't work.

I count to three, and Susan barely gets her chin to the gunwale. I clutch at her life vest and wrestle her up. Craig steadies the boat. I grab her clothes, a belt loop. She is stiff, nearly unconscious, and seems to be mouthing words. When she slithers into the hull I have to manually bend her at the knees to get her under a thwart. She lies on the bottom, pale and distant.

But it is only half done. There is no one to hold a gunwale when Craig comes over the side, and he is half again Susan's weight. This is when we live or die. Right now. The world is in the space between our eyes, here in this canoe, in this charged moment.

Kris perches her weight on the gunwale and leans out on her paddle. I press my knees against the sides of the hull. My face is a foot from Craig's. "Help me," I say, and his eyes hold mine.

We count again; Craig tenses, kicks, and struggles upward. The canoe tips heavily. Kris shouts something incoherent, but I have Craig's belt in my hand, and I pull hard. He dives in face first and twists up along the bottom of the boat next to Susan.

"Jesus! Jesus! Jesus!" I hear myself saying. It seems as if I've been breathing hard for hours. I start fishing in the water for the bow line of their canoe.

"Forget the goddamn boat!" Kris screams.

"No way. I'm not coming back out here!" The thought of another trip terrifies me. When I finally get the rope, I tie it to our stern, and then we are paddling again, towing another anchor, listing heavily to the left.

It isn't until later that I marvel at the fact that we accomplished the rescue, at the daunting physics of dragging a waterlogged, half-dead, 170-pound human being over the side of a canoe in three- and four-foot waves. It isn't until later because we are still fighting for life, still battling wind and water, and two of us are past any hope of saving themselves.

"Talk to her!" I shout to Craig. "Make her respond."

My brother fumbles at Susan's face. He says something slurred and unintelligible. Confused, desperate, cold to the core himself, he tries to give her mouth-to-mouth breathing.

"Craig! Stop. She's breathing okay." Kris has turned around. "Susan! Look at me!"

Her face twitches. Sounds come out of her mouth, but that is all. Kris starts paddling again.

Craig hugs Susan to him in the bottom of the canoe. The lake pitches us forward, and the wind is finally our ally, hurrying us in. I can't imagine anything but this frenzied exertion, this grim panic that has been with us ever since I glanced up and saw their capsized boat an age ago. I have lost my capacity to adjust the pace. When we get to shore, we ram full speed into the rocks, leap into the water, and slide the boat with one heave into the boulders.

Supporting Craig and Susan one at a time, we stumble up a steep bank and into the dense, swampy forest. Kris rips packs apart in search of sleeping bags while I retrieve the second canoe from the waves. It takes both of us to work the two of them out of their wet, heavy clothes; their canvas pants fight back, catching on knees and shoes. We strip ourselves, too, and clamber naked into sleeping bags with them. Then we lie there, suddenly exhausted, hugging the blue-cold bodies of our friends.

The moss is soft and deep beneath us; the air is oddly still, the sound of wind diminished in the trees. I can still feel the lake bucking beneath me, but it is a sunny afternoon again and I refuse to think that our efforts will not be enough.

Susan mumbles something and begins to sob. Kris soothes her and holds her tighter, but she is far off, wrapped in a cold cocoon.

When Craig finally begins to shiver, it wakes me out of a timeless stupor. I have no idea how long we've been lying in the moss, but now his body is burning fuel, exercising to make heat. Soon he's shaking so hard I can barely hold on; his shivers are almost like convulsions.

"Maybe I could eat something," he stammers.

I nurse him with globs of honey on the end of my finger. His muscles work harder. He is grinning with warmth.

But it is a long wait for Susan. She lapses into bouts of sobbing, slips away from us, surfaces briefly. Kris talks to her, coaxes her back, and embraces her unresponsive body. And when she does revive, it is a slow, halting process. Finally she is able to swallow some honey. She begins to shiver. Her eyes kindle with first heat.

Craig rises on his elbow and reaches for her shoulder. "Susan! We're going to live!" His voice is hoarse with emotion, and the image of the two of them draped over the canoe comes stabbing back into my mind. I wonder how far down the path toward reckoning with death they traveled, out there on the relentless lake.

Coming of Age

 It IS A FITFUL NIGHT in the dreary camp on Opacopa Lake, full of waking jolts and scenes replaying, full of forest noises, the wind dying out, and rustling from the other tent. By dawn the lake is calm and bugs are out in force. We patrol the shore and shallow water and find a set of maps, a tarp, and other odds and ends washed in on the waves. All in all we've lost an ax, a frying pan, a fishing pole, and the northern pike.

"Let's paddle to the point for breakfast," Craig suggests. "Maybe there will be a little breeze out there to keep the bugs down."

It is there, as we chew cold cereal, that Craig brings up the possibility of turning around. "We can still get back from here, flag down a train, and get out," he says. "Once we get to the Moisie, there won't be any chance."

A loon pops to the surface in front of us, turns an eye our way, and slides under again. When no one says anything, Craig goes on.

"I've always seen the wilderness in positive terms. It has been where I come for relief, to be alive and strong. But yesterday, for the first time, I understood in more than an intellectual way that it didn't care if I lived or died.

"We lay out there on the canoe, watching you guys paddle away. For a long time we couldn't see you because we were so low in the water. We didn't know if you'd tipped yourselves, whether you'd be back in time to save us.

"Both of us know the signs of hypothermia. The shivering, the slurred speech, when the shivering stopped. We knew we were dying."

Still no one says anything. The suggestion is an enormous one. Turning back, retreating over the same bay, up the little stream, over the divide, and back to the tracks. Waiting there for a train, waving our arms to make it stop, going home. The loon is up again; it burbles quietly. I pick at a scab of lichen, peeling it away from the rock.

"I don't mean to let everyone down," Craig says. "I just want to think about it. We almost died yesterday, and we haven't even gotten to the Moisie yet. I'm afraid now in a way I've never been before."

It is Susan who finally responds. "What if," she says, "we take a lesson from yesterday, and we let that lesson guide the rest of the time? I'm afraid, too, but what if we err on the conservative side from now on?"

There is some current passing back and forth between the two of them, something made up of stubbornness and pride and vulnerability and anger. Although their eyes rarely meet, the conversation, now, is theirs. This is their decision. It is a bigger thing than this journey, than whether to paddle north or south. Bigger by far.

When they're through, we pack away our cereal bowls and get in the canoes. We pick up our paddles and round the point.

A day later I notice the eelgrass being pulled along like hair blowing in an underwater wind. Then the first riffly waves, the constriction of channel. Around a bend the Moisie stretches away, cantering downhill, and the first concussion of rapids beats in the air.

The river materializes out of the necklace of lakes we have crossed, becoming, instantly, a thing of immense power and volume. The water is thundering black amber, dyed with iron, translucent and slick. As we come to shore above a falls, the current clutches at the boat hulls, bumping us toward the brink, a greedy thing. The rapids are a crescendo of endless tons of falling cold water, battered mist, and beaten bedrock. When we gather to discuss this first portage, we have to shout to be heard.

In the brief time since the capsize a poorly concealed dread has crystallized among us. We go about our business, conduct ourselves well, and share stories at the cook fire, but the slightest threat to our control sets the taste of fear in the backs of our throats and makes our voices strident. The capsize came out of nowhere, sudden as a car wreck, and what before had been purely exhilarating and heady and wild now has an edge of terror lurking in it.

"I realized that the wilderness doesn't care if I live or die," Craig had said the morning after the accident. It is a thing we all knew theoretically, but now it is visceral knowledge, infused with vivid mental snapshots—Susan's pale, distant face, serene as death, in the bottom of our canoe; Craig's slurred voice and dull eyes; the capsized yellow boat awash in waves.

At this first rapid the black flies cover us like moving fur. They are the demons of the north, and they are worst along moving water, where they congregate in clouds to lay their eggs on rocks in the current. They make mosquitoes seem dainty and languid by comparison. Our pants are tucked into our socks and we wear long-sleeved shirts and head nets, but the bugs find chinks in our armor, raise welts, and draw blood. Black flies don't sting or bite. They secrete an enzyme that actually eats away skin layers until the blood starts to pool.

We eat a hurried lunch to lessen the pack weight by a few pounds and then scout a route around the rapid. There is no trail besides the occasional caribou tracks, which follow other intentions than ours.

When we return, Kris hefts the first of her two loads, a seventy-pound Duluth pack full of food and kitchen gear. I settle under the canoe. Blackflies cloud around my head in the warm, stagnant air beneath the hull. I am dripping sweat within fifty yards. Kris's feet lead through the cushioned unevenness of sphagnum moss, angular boulder, tree root, and downed log. Craig and Susan are somewhere ahead, out of sight. The route is rougher and seems to go farther inland than I remember, feels longer than expected, but a seventy-five-pound canoe grinding against neck vertebrae always warps a person's perspective.

After a long time Kris stops short and drops her pack. "What the hell?" I hear her mutter. I tip the canoe back so the stern rests on the ground. There is the relief of air against my face and a bewildering view of the Moisie in front of me, flowing the wrong way.

"What the hell is right!" I say, throwing the canoe down in the moss.

It is as if we've been miraculously transported to the opposite bank. Instead of the river being on our right, with the rapid upstream, it is on our left, with an altogether different set of whitewater. Could we be looking at a big tributary? If so, where's the Moisie? I climb to the top of a huge boulder, gaining nothing but a longer view of this mystery drainage and no sign of the Moisie.

What we have forgotten, under the duress of insect panic, with the passage of time, and in the state of mind brought on by the capsize—that condition of insecurity and fear in which things can go fatally awry in a heartbeat—is that the portage was along the right side of an island that the Moisie splits around. Instead of carrying along the right channel, we have actually crossed the island and now confront the left branch of the Moisie, with its unique set of roiling water.

I have my hands on my hips and a look of stunned bewilderment on my face. Kris points downstream as if to explain the predicament, but her voice trails off and her arm drops. We turn to each other. Through the lens of a video camera we would look hilariously confused, but we are absolutely baffled. What the hell is going on? Should we try to retrace our steps? Should we follow the "tributary" until we make sense of this? If we leave our load to go and reconnoiter, will we ever find it again? Where are Craig and Susan?

At a loss, we start to yell and whistle, hoping for rescue. Our voices sound thin and strained. The rapids thunder in the background.

"Behind you," I hear Craig's voice say. He and Susan are standing on a boulder looking down on us.

"You guys looked as if you'd landed on Mars," he says when we explain our confusion. "Didn't you remember we were on an island?"

In its first thirty-five miles the Moisie drops at the rate of thirty feet per mile. A river gradient of twenty feet per mile is considered to be pushing the envelope for open canoes. Percussive falls; frothy, rock-lined chasms; and long stair steps of ledges punctuate the route with wearying frequency. We encounter this maelstrom of headlong flow saddled with our self-doubt, with a capsized sense of our abilities, even with the menacing thought that this wild descent is something more than impartial, a place we need to survive.

For days we are out of the canoes, portaging through the fog of black flies, more than we are on the river. It is a mark of my overriding preoccupation, my obsession with our struggle, and of my physical exhaustion that in all this time I don't write a single word in my trip journal. It is as if I can't afford the luxury of reflection or the lapse in concentration.

As much as a mile above an approaching rapid we start to hug the shoreline and backpaddle around corners, on guard against surprise. Again and again the landings for portages seem perched at the very brinks of waterfalls, in the steady, deadly din of sound where mist wets the air and the water has that serene, smooth, no-going-back-now certainty about it.

Only periodically do we find established portage trails. Often as not we bushwhack through black spruce, willow, and alder thickets, our feet sucking into bog muck, or clamber over deadfall, our faces whipped by vegetation, picking up and then losing game trails. The packs and canoes are awkward, spine-torquing baggage. Black fly bites make us look like boxers on the short end of the scorecard. They puff our eyelids half shut, swell our lips, and make our ear lobes bleed. At lunch stops we laugh at one another's new wounds. In the tent at night Kris and I take inventory of our scabs.

Craig and Susan are not reconciled by this journey or by their intense experience with hypothermia. We never hear them talking in their tent. The capsize was a thing they survived together, but their relationship remains strained and tight. Kris and I discuss strategy in the canoe almost constantly, but Craig and Susan are either silent or arguing.

When, infrequently, we gain a bit of our paddling confidence back with a good run, we are slapped down again by some mishap. In the midst of a fun stretch of whitewater, a lurking mid-river hole suddenly appears downstream. Kris's voice is immediately on the verge of panic. Backpaddle as we might, we are sucked on toward the throat of water with its snarling wave. We just manage to avoid the center of the hole but are struck a glancing blow by a wave that drops twenty gallons of river over the bow.

And again, along a tricky bit of river that we elect to negotiate from a low rock ledge above the water, lining the boats along with ropes attached to bow and stern. Craig and Susan go first, controlling their loaded boat from ten feet above. All goes well until, near the end, the bow nudges around a small point of rock, the stern gets a bit far into the current, and, quick as the thought, the canoe swamps.

The Moisie is a grand and wild river—two hundred miles of dark, unfettered power pouring off the iron-hardened land, majesty beyond words—but nestled in at the heart of my embrace of that wildness is a lump of dread that has solidified and settled, leaden and dark, like an infidelity between lovers.

Along the middle segment of the watercourse, more than a week after the capsize, the flow starts to moderate. There are a few pooled, quiet sections where the current pauses, mixed with some long, heady gallops where the bottom whips past at a dizzying rate and we all grin with the speed. Bedrock walls lift one and two thousand feet above the valley, great rock expanses as smooth and exfoliated as the heights of Yosemite. Scars from recent fires brand the landscape in ragged, gaping patterns, shadow plays of gray ash and black trunks.

We pass through one spot that is the eeriest place I have ever been on the water. In that momentary passage I feel exactly the way I remember feeling as a young boy one night on the Atlantic shore. That night I walked down through the meadow in front of my grandparents' house to the edge of the ocean, then out to the end of a wooden dock, and sat there, legs dangling over the black water. It was so dark I couldn't make out the gentle waves but only heard them heaving solemnly through the pilings, feeling them beneath me. There, in the night, as I hung over the abyss, the mystery and fathomless power of the ocean, its compelling implacability, curled up around me with such seductive strength that it was all I could do to grip the splintery wood and not pitch forward into its arms.

The spooky moment on the Moisie is a pinch in the channel after a long, quiet pool, a constriction so tight that I have the mistaken impression that I could reach out and touch either wall with my paddle. It is not that tight, but it's near enough. The weird thing is that at such a narrows there is no rapid. The canoe hull is a thin husk on the black, glassy water. How deep must this be, I am wondering. Kris and I say nothing. I lift my paddle clear, as if there are things I don't want to encounter beneath the surface.

There is no rapid, yet the river is not calm, either. It gurgles through this rocky neck, jostling and unpredictable. Blisters of water burst upward in slow motion, methodical and constrained as lava, slow boils that turn the canoes in quarter circles. The rock shackles the river, but it feels tenuous as hell. Our ride through can't be more than a few seconds long. When the channel widens again and the river resumes its predictable, more familiar motion, I realize that I have been holding my breath.

Near the end, two weeks after our capsize on Opacopa Lake, we come to a final major piece of whitewater where the Moisie runs parallel to a set of train tracks and then makes a sharp turn under a high-trestle railroad bridge. The trip is nearly done, and the temptation to run this rollicking stretch is great. At the beginning of it we lift the canoes over a small ledge and cluster together to consider the river.

Just in front of where I'm standing, the Moisie pours smoothly over a ragged lip of rock. The water, rushing past, is a clear, seamless, molten arc, and the rock beneath is cast in unwavering amber light. It is both lovely and hypnotizing, breathtaking and sinister—a beautiful, unimaginable strength passing two steps away.

We decide that it will be best to sneak and line down the less turbulent water alongshore. Susan's cautionary advice the morning after the capsize is still fresh. Choosing caution, in fact, has become our dogma.

Even the timid route turns out to be pretty exciting, involving some tricky maneuvering past boulders and in and out of eddies. Once, as we skirt a point of rock, I glance midriver. Ten feet away there are standing waves surging up well above my head.

Just before the river turns ninety degrees to pass under the train bridge, there is a short section that we decide to wade with the boats alongshore. We are in the river up to our waists, feeling our way over the underwater boulders, embraced by the iron flow, when the stern line we are unwittingly trailing gets hung up. The canoe stops abruptly, tugging against the nylon rope.

I haul on the line, but it won't give. We shove the canoe back upstream until I am above the snag. For five minutes I yank from every possible angle, even submerging myself neck deep in search of the place where the rope is caught, to no avail.

Craig hands me his knife from where he is standing onshore. I pull a few more times, as if this mysterious impediment is something personal and insulting that I don't want to capitulate to, one last thing the river wants to claim. Then I reach well underwater and saw on the taut rope until it breaks.

We go on toward the finish, toward our larger lives, but the length of white nylon stays, whipping endlessly, eel-like, in the dark river.

Partner

FROM THE RAILROAD YARD in Sept-Îles, Quebec, near the mouth of the Moisie River, I drove directly to my job at Northland College in northern Wisconsin, with the canoe strapped to the top of my car. Kris and I separated at O'Hare Airport in Chicago. We would see each other over the years, we never had a falling out to point to, but from that moment our lives slid apart.

Almost a year later, on a Friday during spring semester, I pass Grant between buildings on the Northland campus. He is a colleague with whom I work closely in the Outdoor Education program. More important, he is an avid and gifted paddler.

"I just heard that the Montreal is running at thirteen hundred cfs," Grant says. "Supposed to stay up through Sunday."

The Montreal is a river that claims a brief geographic life but makes a frothing glory of it. The stream piles down the side of the enormous, ice-scoured crucible that once held glacial Lake Duluth and that still holds the shrunken greatness of Lake Superior. It is barely fifty miles long, running the border between northern Wisconsin and the upper peninsula of Michigan, and its flow is truncated by the indignity of a dam.

Much of the year the Montreal is unpaddleable, a tortured, dewatered course of boulder and ledge and narrow defile. Every so often, though, a window opens—after a torrential rain, sometimes, or when the dam managers release an uncommon slug of water. Then, briefly, the Montreal is an unparalleled whitewater joy. That ragged, unpredictable pulse of possibility is a rhythm monitored by a small, avid society of local paddlers. When the Montreal is up, a few offices close in Ironwood, Michigan; some college students skip class in Ashland, Wisconsin; appointments are rescheduled in Hurley.

By nine o'clock Saturday morning Grant's sixteen-foot whitewater canoe is lashed on top of my blue pickup, the eroded muffler has been rewired to the chassis, and we are sipping coffee from a thermos on our way to the put-in.

An hour later we leave the truck parked in a riverside weed bed and settle into the canoe. There is that palpable aura common to the beginnings of all great whitewater pitches—an emanation that is a churning mixture of heated joy, accelerated heart rates, constricted bowels, anxious hands on paddle grips, and a lurking fear that we do our best to ignore. It is a moment of abandon and anticipation balanced so tentatively against the possibility of failure and mishap that a single reasonable excuse to give it up might deflate the whole enterprise. Then the stern of the canoe breaks away from the mud bank, the boat enters the current, and we are at once as vulnerable and as self-reliant as a space module separating from the parent ship.

Within a mile we endure the anticlimax of a portage along a railroad bed. The carry gets us past a section of narrow rock gorge full of pounding water and to a place, just below, where we can put back in at the top of a long stretch of fast, bouldery river.

Grant kneels in the bow. He is close enough, in the small boat, for me to tap on the shoulder with my paddle blade. We have discussed the first few moves through the rocky maze, plotting a vague line to follow, but beyond that the run will be a choreography of snap judgments, of spontaneous responses to wave and eddy, to each other's strokes, to the shifting hull—a rumba of the synapses.

We begin. I paddle on the left, Grant on the right. Ten strokes downriver the pace settles in, slow-motion and fluid, focused like a spotlight: a communication between flowing water, boat hull, and two human beings. The Montreal requires both aggression and finesse, boldness and acquiescence. We plunge down a tight slot between boulders and ride the plume of smooth water below it; slow ourselves to the speed of the river to coast through a set of standing waves; back-ferry a third of the river's width to skirt a reef of cobbles the size of bowling balls; make two quick half pivots to avoid a dead-ahead boulder; rest for three beats, paddles poised above the river, and then dig in through a wave, Grant powering forward while I lean out on my paddle for balance.

We speak hardly a word. Grant points ahead with his paddle and I see his strategy; he drives in a sharp, fast draw stroke and at the same moment I pry in the stern briefly to sideslip a lurking rock. He starts to backpaddle, straining against the strokes, and I angle the stern to ferry across the current; he digs in through a recirculating wave and I hang out hard on a high brace. Bend after bend it goes on. The action is so unrelieved that we get winded by it. The only way to rest is to grab a narrow eddy alongshore and cling to the vegetation, breathing hard, laughing.

Somewhere—say, a third of the way along—we recognize

without a word that this is one of those magic runs, a time when everything works, when the fibrous water and the responsive boat and the telepathy between us can't go wrong. A time when we know what the river is asking, and we know we can do it. To announce this awareness would be to stop it, so we guard it, stay centered in it, concentrate it.

There is one four-foot plunge at a sheer ledge that we take down the deepest notch of water, a braid of the river we ride over the drop. There are diagonal waves curling over sheets of rock that we punch through. There are boisterous constrictions, unavoidable drops, fields of rock, piling masses of current, and dancing holes where we turn upstream and surf, suspended in the roar of passing water that sounds, just then, like applause.

The boat is something we wear, a thing the two of us put on like clothing. In it we become a single entity joined in motion. The luscious, accelerating spin of an eddy turn. The three-step waltz past a car-sized boulder. The breath-held plummet down a slick chute. The tiptoe tension along a thin thread of water piercing through boiling conflict.

At the end we stand on solid ground again, grinning at each other like fools, but the river is still pounding down the nerve lines. I am awake half that night replaying the Montreal running under the hull.

W<small>HAT HAS REMAINED SHARP</small> and crystalline from my years in the upper Midwest is the time spent paddling with Grant. We worked closely together at the college, planned curricula, led trips, socialized, and became best friends, but the purest expression of our energy coalesced around boats and moving water. It wasn't so much the frequency or number of our trips that I remember as the purity and fierceness of our interaction on them.

That passion led us down rivers so late in the fall that we had to break through half an inch of ice at the take-out and so early in the spring that if we capsized, we had to clamber up three feet of ice still clinging to the riverbanks. We paddled rivers at flood stage, at bony low water, under the moon. We snuck down creeks barely big enough to turn around in and stroked across strings of mirrored lakes livid with fall colors.

It was like finding that great dance partner with whom, when you slide onto the open floor, you create a kind of luminosity by your movements together. For us the floor was the shifting, dynamic fall of water rolling downhill, the music was the chords of current playing off rock and ledge and moss bank, and our silent collaborators were the boats we wore.

Our boating partnership peaked with the purchase of a C-2 from a friend in Green Bay. To the uninitiated, a C-2 looks pretty much like a kayak with two cockpits. It is, in fact, a covered canoe in which the paddlers kneel, wearing neoprene skirts to cover the cockpit holes. As in a canoe, boaters in a C-2 stroke on opposite sides with single-bladed paddles. These craft are made for moving water, for serious racing and tight maneuvering on whitewater that only fools or Olympians would attempt in an open canoe. They are the Lamborghinis of the canoeing world.

The one we bought was a low-volume design, which is to say that it looked like a slightly thickened surfboard tapered to sharp points. At first glance the idea that two largish people could kneel inside the hull seemed physically impossible, but Grant and I crimped our way into the tight cockpits like people wiggling into clothes from a thinner era. Within two minutes we understood the essence of life in a C-2—a blend of exquisite pain, arising from the fact that you are essentially sitting on your heels with legs folded at acute angles and the tops of your feet flat against the boat hull, and intense pleasure, derived from the sweet, responsive motion of a sleek boat riding an inch or two above the water. In the C-2 we wore not only the boat, but also the river.

On the drive home from Green Bay we succumbed to temptation at a small roadside rapid called Gilmore's Mistake on the Wolf River. We entered the C-2 in our street clothes and experienced about forty-five sweet seconds of wearing the river before we capsized crossing into an eddy.

Our C-2 career was like that, throughout. Moments of pain, excruciating glory, and ignoble defeat, in equal measure. Forty-five minutes in the boat was about as long as we could endure the torture at a stretch before one of us gave in and requested a stop. Onshore, we hauled ourselves from the boat in exactly the fashion in which paraplegics haul themselves out of wheelchairs. Then for several minutes we massaged our ankles, waited for the hot pain of renewed blood flow, and hobbled in circles, leaning on our paddles.

The C-2 was not a craft we chose for quiet lakeshore paddles or lazy flat-water bits of river. The only reason to fall prey to its peculiar anguish was to taste the ecstasy that must be a lot like driving a tiny, uncomfortable car at 150 miles per hour.

Ecstasy like the moment we experienced on the Brule River. We were about an hour and a half into the day, which meant that we'd already dragged the lifeless lower halves of our bodies out of the boat twice and were on the still-sentient cusp of another downriver leg.

Across the way a ledge jutted several feet into the river, with a watery surfing hole beneath it. When a river plunges over a large rock or ledge, creating a hole in the surface of the current, there is always a wave on the downstream side. In strong current those waves are so steep that they crest at the top, breaking back on themselves. These curlers are sometimes big enough to balance a boat on. Because the wave is breaking back on itself, upstream, you can, in theory, paddle up to just the right place and the wave will hold the boat there, stationary, teetering amid the flow of current. It is a heady moment when it happens right.

We turned the C-2 to face upstream and paddled over toward the curler, inching our way into the froth from river left. On an average surfing wave the boat will be held in precarious balance for five or ten seconds before finally slipping off. On a better-than-average surf the powerful wave will first pull the bow down into the water and then start to submerge it while you remain balanced in the flow. On an outrageous surfing wave the entire front third of the boat, along with the bow paddler, can get taken slowly but forcefully under while the stern paddler rises clear of the water.

At first contact this one felt like a better-than-average wave, with the potential to turn outrageous. We climbed up it, surfed, and fell off several times. On the final try the bow began planing under, deeper and deeper, until Grant was up to his rib cage in the river. Then, instead of the stern rising clear, the back end of the boat began submerging as well, in a wave just behind me. In slow motion the C-2 went down, first the bow and then the stern, until we realized that we were actually kneeling on the bedrock at the river bottom, with the Brule rushing past at our shoulders. Finally, the boat slowly broke free and rose, swaying from side to side, to pop out of the spell.

Despite the exhilaration of paddling the C-2, traditional canoes remained the dominant craft in our outings. Time on the water did for us what Friday-night happy hours seemed to do for most of the working population of northern Wisconsin.

One summer night after we hadn't seen each other for

weeks, we arranged to meet at a lonely intersection somewhere on the Bayfield Peninsula and struck off together on
the back roads, as receptive to inspiration as teenagers cruising the strip.

Until midnight we roamed the country roads within a
forty-mile radius, drank Leinenkugels out of dark, long-
necked bottles, and listened to the Allman Brothers on the
tape deck. About then the night might have died off satis-
factorily, except that one of us brought up the possibility of
paddling the White River.

The project faltered momentarily over the logistics of our
vehicle shuttle, but we decided to ignore that aspect of the
arrangement. Something would work out. If worse came to
worst, we could always hike the six miles back to the truck.
By one o'clock in the morning we were stumbling around
and untying the canoe in a dirt lot next to a power station at
the base of a dam.

The night was so black that we couldn't even make each
other out in the canoe. In that humid summer impenetrabil-
ity we could have been on the Amazon or the Congo. The
forest overhung the slow river; insects droned in a wavering
monotone; the boat bumped up against half-submerged logs
and scraped under tree trunks. Grant balanced on the bow
plate, facing backward, while I reclined against the stern
plate.

Two bends downriver the frenetic pace of the evening fell
away. We stopped talking. On the whispering current a
beaver slapped water like a pistol shot five feet away. Animals
rustled off through the underbrush or watched us pass with
disembodied, glowing eyes. The White coiled with languid
force through the tepid, pregnant night. Dew beaded up like
rain in the grass.

What had been an aimless evening full of the brute electricity of companionship had become something distilled,

calm, heartfelt, a sightless feeling our way down a summer-held river, bound together by the hull of a canoe. In the blackness, just this: two of us in a boat, invisible to each other, with a river unfurling beneath.

Solo

THE EASIEST WAY to paddle a canoe solo is to turn a tandem boat backward and sit in the bow seat, facing the stern. By doing so, the paddler is positioned nearly in the center of the canoe, and is better able to control the boat. There is no need to buy a separate, solo boat for solitary trips, no need to make customized foam saddles, install thigh straps, or glue D-rings to the hull. Just turn the boat around, get in, and paddle off.

There is a forest-fire haze in the July sky when I turn my boat backward and set out alone into the English River country of central Ontario. The usually cloudless blue is grimy as a city skyline. Canada has the feel of Arizona this summer, as if all the bush is dried-up tinder, brittle pine duff.

I have a week. I want to be by myself. My work at the college puts me in the field with groups of students more than one hundred days per year. When I am not in the wilds with students, I am advising them in my office, signing forms, attending committee meetings, and justifying proposals to the academic dean. My need for this escape has burgeoned into an insistent yearning, an urge close to panic, a need both longed for and feared. Can I still be content with myself?

I have driven north around the western rim of Lake Superior, on north and west, past the Boundary Waters and Quetico crowds. I had no idea where I would end up. At a Natural Resources office in Dryden I settled on a circle-shaped loop of lakes and rivers and picked up maps. No one knows where I am.

It is hot and windless, the deerflies are biting, and I break a sweat in the gravel parking lot getting myself organized. Once on the water, only twenty yards offshore, with the noise of traffic still in the air, I already feel quite alone. The feeling, at the start, is of both exultation and sadness.

A short distance down the lakeshore I nose the canoe into a small creek and start up against the current. The water is shallow, pushier than it looks, and the channel is a narrow, twisting slot through weed beds. The canoe weaves and jerks in response to my strokes; the hull squeezes through a bristling breach in an old beaver dam and then glides with satisfying ease across the quiet water above. The channel opens into another lake. It is a looking-glass passage; the parking lot, the smell of car fumes, the picnic-table flies, all less than a mile away, have vanished.

I shift from my knees up to the canoe seat and notice the breeze coming down the lake because it is pushing the light end of the canoe off course. I heave one of the packs far forward to help trim the boat and start to paddle on the off-wind side. The canoe strikes a balance between wind resistance and my paddling momentum, so we move slightly crabwise down the shore.

I am alone. I say this, internally, in time with my strokes. Alone. Alone. Alone. It is a thing I need to assert, to work at attaining. I am not alone comfortably. I am not free of the habit of conversation, diversion, the clutter of people. The wind is freshening all the time, roughening the lake with small chops, the canoe's angle becomes more and more crablike. It is good to focus on the effort, as if exertion and sweat might purge the awkwardness of transition.

On the first portage trail I work myself hard, half jogging with the pack over the rough path and not allowing myself a break from the canoe grinding against my neck. When I reach the far side, I dunk my sweaty head in a pool. When was the last time I spent a day without speaking? How long has it been since I spent eight waking hours without bumping into a human? Why, even now, do I cast everything in terms of sharing this with someone, having stories to tell?

When I stroke away from shore, moving farther into the country, I have a new mantra. Be here, I say. Be here. Be here. Be here. Be here. At the end of the day I am still foreign, as if I have been pinned onto the landscape like a colored flag on a map. I slip off to the tent early, the sun an hour or two from the horizon, because I have done everything I can think of and am tired of sitting still.

On the second day, with the sun high overhead, I scout another portage trail around a rapid. Partway across I leave the path and work through the brush toward the noise of whitewater. First I study the rocky constriction to see how I might run it in the canoe. I could do this, I think, though I know I won't. My eyes ride the current, moving down a tongue, past the edge of a ledge, into an eddy, across to a pool, and out the final train of waves. With a partner I'd go in a shot, but it is not a chance I'll take alone.

Then I move onto a sun-washed, water-smoothed point, fast water at my toes, and sit down. I take off my boots and rest my pale feet against the warm, rust-colored stone. A whitethroat sings behind me. Canada, I think. I could be blindfolded and dropped out of an airplane, but if there were whitethroats singing their straight-ahead tune, I'd know it was summer in the north country.

I close my eyes. The drumming water comes through the rock and into the soles of my feet. The air is charged with the sound. I am pulled into the funnel of noise, pummeled by it, full of it, as if the beat of water and rock has taken over the work of my heart.

Maybe I sit there for a long time; maybe it is only a few moments. I have no idea, but when I rise again, the internal mantra is gone, replaced by the uncluttered authority of a whitethroat and the blood rush of falling water.

Time becomes less and less the dictate I impose on the days. My watch ticks in the glove compartment of my truck. The band of untanned skin on my wrist blends, day by day, with the freckled, summer-weathered skin around it. There are other, more immediate measures to go by—the shoulder ache of a twenty-mile day, the drowsiness of midafternoon, the hunger of a two-lake, one-portage morning—and eighteen hours of sun besides. More and more I am woven into the pattern of place and season. A tern tilts above the head-high reeds along a lazy, tight-coiled stretch of water. The cattails and rushes clatter to jabs of wind.

Three days running, afternoon winds shove the canoe sideways, kick up waves, and blow me against riverbanks. Along one protected corner of willowy shore, a restful, windless sanctuary, a cow moose erupts out of the thickets. Her velvet tan nose quivers at arm's length. Deerflies cling to her ears; muck rises up past her bony knees. Although she is rigidly still, the loose skin under her neck sways back and forth as we look each other over.

Then she plunges along the riverbank next to the canoe, in water to her chest, knees rising clear out of the spray. She runs like this long enough to leave an impression of confusion and fear before she finds an alley into the brush and disappears. The sounds she makes, crashing off, last only a few seconds.

In the tent one night at an island camp I make a resolution to rise when I hear the first bird sing at daybreak. Partly this is a strategy to avoid the afternoon winds. Mostly it's a strange desire to be about at dawn. I am brought awake by a sound in the pitch blackness and lie there, listening for it again: a subdued twitter, answered from the other side of the tent. The horizon is barely gray, stars are still out, and the air is cold, but I dress and start the small stove to boil water for coffee while I pack.

When I slide the canoe down a polished ramp of bedrock into the lake, the hull enters the water as if it is tearing through satin, ripping it without a sound. And when I slip away in the cool, gray light toward a dim point of land, it is as if I am pulling a long tear through sheer, tense fabric behind me.

In half a mile I move from night to day. Mist coils off the sparkling water and hangs in the backs of coves in small clouds. I close my eyes and keep stroking. I think that I would like to know what it's like to paddle blind, really blind, so that this travel would be more swimming than riding and day would be only the warmth on my face and a diffuse glow in the darkness.

When I open my eyes, a great blue heron shifts in the weeds and then freezes, still as a stick. A northern pike, as much snake as fish, weaves away into the weeds under the canoe's shadow. For a while I chase a loon around a cove, trying to guess where it will pop up next. The red-eyed bird seems to join in the game. Once she comes up, sleek and shining, very close by, and I see that she is carrying a downy chick on her back.

Farther along there is rock art under an overhang on a low

cliff that falls sheer into the lake. It seems to me the kind of thing one would work at in the fall, on a warm, still day after a frost, when winter is coming on with its kind of death and the urge to make one's mark rises up irresistibly. I stand in my canoe at the base of the gray-red rock and place my hands against its cold, weathered hardness.

In the afternoon the winds, for once, don't come up. The water is a platinum stillness in the heat. I am drowsy. My head nods and I jerk awake. How can I fall asleep while I'm paddling, I think. I slip to my knees to reach a more stable position in case I do.

I think about home to keep my eyelids open. I picture the house I rent, in the small Wisconsin town with more bars than are legal, with its green front porch and bowed-out walls. I see the friends I go dancing with on Saturday nights. I list the classes I teach and the courses for next semester. I dredge up the faces of students, visualize the way the college president strides across campus between meetings.

All of it is utterly familiar and yet absolutely strange. I have been on the water only a week, but the images that come to me are more than distant; they are unconnected. This place I have entered, where I have come alone, has no point of contact with that place. I have slipped gears and landed in another dimension. Conjuring my other life is an exercise in abstraction.

Here on this hot, shiny lake, alone in a canoe, I am still drowsy. I think what a fool I'd feel if I dozed off and tipped out of the boat.

Part II

The Main Stem

Rebounding Land

IMAGINE THE WEIGHT. During the glacial age, just yesterday if you think like a rock, the ice cap must have squatted on what is now Hudson Bay with the weight of a mountain range. Two miles thick, more than 10,000 feet of compacted snow and ice built up over millennia of climatic chill. Imagine the groaning, elastic flow; the encircling clutch around rocks the size of Cadillacs, the rasping force, polishing bedrock, gouging basins, and rounding hills.

From here the ice pulsed across the continent repeatedly for a million and a half years, dozing the holes for Lake Superior, Lake Winnipeg, Great Slave Lake, and Lake Athabasca. It throbbed slowly back and forth, unleashing cataclysmic floods, eroding land like a garden hose in a sandbox, migrating with boulders, building topography and then planing it flat again.

The last of the perennial ice finally melted away here, at Hudson Bay, some ten thousand years ago. The land, relieved of a burden it shouldered for a good portion of the

Pleistocene, is still rebounding, as if heaving a slow geologic sigh. The earth's rigid crust rides with sluggish buoyancy on the molten mantle beneath it. Where there is a greater weight, as beneath a mountain range or under an ice cap, the crust sinks more deeply into the mantle. When the weight is removed, by the erosion of mountains or the melting of ice, the crust is buoyed upward in response. Measurements indicate that the Hudson Bay region is rising roughly an inch every year and that it has already bounced back more than 1,000 feet. Geologists estimate that it may still have 2,000 feet to go.

Another legacy of the ice cap is a landscape scraped so flat, a plane so slightly inclined, that the gap between high and low tide can be five miles wide. The shoreline of Hudson Bay north of the port of Churchill, Manitoba, is a demarcation where high tide gives way to low, mossy ground stretching away to a fuzzy meeting with sky.

Rivers like the Seal, the Knife, and the Thlewiaza feed into the ocean through fields of glacially mauled boulders. As we paddle the last fast shallows on the Seal River, the scent of salt, an unhindered breeze, and a sense of impending spaciousness waft upstream. We have been traveling across northern Manitoba for nearly a month. I am with Grant and several other friends in three canoes, and it is my first journey with Marypat.

So intent are we on finishing the river and crossing the ocean threshold that we don't notice the polar bear until it has slipped down the bank and into the water and is swimming toward us. Nor do we feel particularly threatened even then, except that it soon becomes apparent that the bear is investigating us. Its coat is a slightly yellowed white; its head is broad as an anvil. Marypat has the camera out and is snapping pictures. The bear moves languidly, ponderously, but with such fluid power, such confident grace, and such surprising speed that the effect is hypnotic.

I shake free enough of the spell to get Marypat to stow the camera. Then we backpaddle in against a muddy point of land and join the other canoes. The six of us clump together onshore while the white bear patrols back and forth at twenty feet. We can hear it breathe, taking in our scent. For ten minutes it pins us there and we watch each other. Several times the bear rises so that its broad shoulders are out of the water, the better to assess us. We shout at the animal and clang pots, with no discernible effect. The bear comes no closer, but neither does it back away or waver in its focus.

Finally, the bear's interest seems to wane. It swims slowly to one side, near the riverbank, far enough away that we feel able to make a dash for the next short rapid. We climb carefully into the boats, push off together, and stroke quickly across the pool. The bear turns back toward us, but we are already into the fast water, shooting away downstream. When we look back up from the calm water below, the polar bear is watching from the head of the rapid, perched half out of the water on a broad rock.

This is my first expedition to the Far North since the fateful journey on the Moisie, three years ago. Marypat and I had met six months earlier at my brother's courtroom wedding in Evanston, Wyoming. Southwestern Wyoming was in the throes of an oil boom, and there was a kind of brute, metallic energy there, a subdued frenzy as tangible as a coming rain. There weren't enough carts at the grocery store or enough mailboxes at the post office. On payday the line at the bank coiled around the block. People were asked to check their guns before entering bars.

In the short time we spent together, little more than a week, we fell in love under the cloud of that energy. We danced to western swing bands in bars jammed with transients. Marypat smuggled champagne into the courtroom for the wedding. For the next six months we carried on a torrid long-distance relationship punctuated by several visits and dozens of hours with telephones smeared to our ears. At the end of the school year I moved to Montana to be with her. It was a move based on passion and geography: passion for Marypat and for the West. Despite the good work and strong friendships that had come my way in Wisconsin, I had never shaken the sense that I was marooned in a geography that wasn't home.

Marypat is an accomplished outdoorswoman and a strong athlete, but she had never paddled a canoe before this journey. She has picked up canoeing skills over these weeks of lake and river paddling through northern Manitoba. She is already a competent and intuitive canoeist whose only shortcoming is a zest for excitement that regularly overwhelms her better judgment. I tell her that she needs a capsize or two to work up a proper sense of caution.

Around a bend the small sea opens before us. The canoes enter, abruptly dwarfed by the expanse. We have no idea what stage the tides are in, but the strategy we have agreed on is to paddle only at high tide. Since the water at low ebb recedes so far from shore, our concern is that if we were to follow it out, by the time high tide returned the weather conditions might have shifted, or an offshore gale might prevent us from coming back in.

There are thousands of snow geese and Canada geese at the mouth of the river. We watch one group running around onshore flapping wings wildly, squawking, and rushing back and forth as if herded by winds. Then we see a black wolf in their midst, a tall, lean animal feinting through the flurry of wings. The wolf singles out a white snow goose, grabs it by the neck, and trots off. The geese across the way start a similar commotion, and we watch another wolf, this one tawny white, chase down its quarry. The geese are molting so heavily that they are unable to fly, and the wolves are no fools. Before we paddle on, a third wolf has given chase along another section of the shore.

From the boats it is impossible to tell exactly where the water stops and dry land starts. We are hundreds of yards out, and our paddles still routinely hit bottom. It's very clear when the tide goes out, though, because it's as if someone has pulled the bathtub plug. Water flows in sudden currents around rocks and we turn in toward land, paddling as hard as we can, but make barely fifty feet before the boats are firmly aground. Within fifteen minutes the line of receding water is out of sight. There seems to be very little life in the rubble, few plants, no crabs scuttling around, no brackish ooze, just rocks and sand and our stranded outfit.

When evening settles and we've eaten dinner, we discuss strategy. Our combined intelligence about tidal patterns is exhausted in minutes. We set watch alarms at various intervals, spread sleeping bags on the lumpy rocks next to the boats, and turn in. There are no insects this far from shore, so we sleep under the stars.

The forty-mile stint on Hudson Bay has been the preoccupation of this month in the Manitoba bush. In hundreds of paddling miles it has been these last couple of days that loomed over it all. For weeks we have navigated through the transitional country between forest and tundra, seeing no one. We have run rapids at the edge of our ability, portaged between drainages, and paddled through storms, but never once have we forgotten that to end the journey, we will have to cross forty miles of open ocean.

Hudson Bay is a place of remarkable tides, where winter recedes for less than three months every year and polar bears roam the river deltas. Not a place, particularly, for canoes. But the mouth of the Seal is just north of Churchill; on the map it didn't look far. Now we are here, dropped on the moonscape of intertidal rubble, with an August night coming on.

Before I drift off, I remember a story a friend once told me. He had traveled extensively on the shores of Hudson

Bay and spent many nights camped on tidal flats. One night he slept without a tent because the bugs were light, just as we are doing tonight. When he woke in the morning and opened his eyes, a polar bear was sniffing his face from six inches away. The bear's breath may, in fact, have been what woke him. His response was to close his eyes tight. When he next opened them, the bear was shambling away in the distance.

I am lying next to Marypat, the canoe nearby. These weeks have been a kind of honeymoon for our partnership. We don't know it yet, but the next decade will be full of northern honeymoons, thousands of miles spent in boats together, and our relationship will be forged and defined by experiences on the water.

It is pitch black when I open my eyes. Marypat is shaking me roughly. "Quick! Get up. The tide's coming." She trots off to rouse the rest of the group. I notice green sheets of northern lights waving through the stars of the Big Dipper, and then I see the glint of water just past the stern of the canoe. I have time to stuff my sleeping bag in its sack, throw it in the canoe with the packs, and hop in before the water lifts the boat off the rocks.

My companions are invisible in the darkness. I hear the rustle of sleeping bag fabric, the dull thump of shoes against canoe hull, breathless snatches of conversation.

When the water is deep enough, we paddle toward shore through the minefield of boulders and then turn south. The lights of Churchill glow eerily against the sky, forty miles away. The ocean is calm, the night moonless. We all have to keep talking to one another to stay together. Marypat's and my boat gets stuck on a rock, and by the time we're free I can't hear the rest of the group. I call out for them, my voice charged with irrational panic.

Finally, the water is deep enough that we can stay clear of

rocks and stick together. For long periods the splashes our paddles make are the only breaks in the quiet. Invisible flocks of ducks fly past us, just over the water, their wings whispering through the chill air. Eider ducks, I think, because they sound muffled and warm, but they could be anything.

It is our blind good fortune that the wind wasn't up when the tide came in. We would have slammed around in the rocks and surf, lost contact with one another, and holed our hulls. Hudson Bay is littered with the wreckage of boats that foundered in its shoals in rough weather. Just a year earlier four canoeists were lost near here in a sudden storm, their boats smashed to fragments in fifteen-foot waves. Some of the bodies were never recovered. A journal that washed ashore documented group tensions, food supplies that had run out, and a series of poor decisions that had culminated in the group's taking a terminal shortcut across the mouth of Button Bay on a windy day. Churchill was almost in sight when they died.

Hudson Bay itself is named after an early explorer who lost his life here. Henry Hudson made four attempts to discover a Northwest Passage to the Orient. On one journey he sailed as far south as the Hudson River, leaving his name behind, and on two others he struck north into the Arctic ice pack. His final attempt concentrated on this dead-end oceanic embayment in the years 1610 and 1611.

Sailing the fifty-five-ton *Discovery,* Hudson spent the summer of 1610 bumping along the eastern coast of the bay, all the way south to the bottom of James Bay and back north along the western coast, casting about for an opening. When winter struck, the crew forted up for an arduous, starving season on the western shore. By all accounts, relations among the men were already strained. The winter was spent bickering over food supplies and feuding over the small matters that loom so large in confined quarters. By spring the tensions had become insurmountable.

Once under sail again in June 1611, the mutinous crew set Hudson, his son, and seven men adrift in a small boat. They were never heard from again. Twenty years later explorers Luke Fox and Thomas James, whose names adorn other regional features, discovered the ruins of a primitive encampment that they speculated may have been Hudson's.

Today the weather stays calm for us. The sun rises, huge and red, through low bands of cloud. The surface of the ocean is a dull slate blue. We paddle as close to shore as we can until we sense the tide shifting, and then we sprint in to a beach near the Knife River's outlet.

For two days our routine is tethered to the tides. When the water is in, we paddle, day or night. When it is out, we prepare meals, play cards, nap, and walk inland. The impression is one of compressed time, and every day is made up of two abbreviated daily cycles.

One more time we are caught by low tide some distance from shore, and have to wait, reclined in the canoes, while the flats dry out enough for us to trudge across to the beach. Hours later the distant line of water reappears and we hurry back to the canoes, where we wait to lift off.

Although it is still calm when we arrive at the mouth of Button Bay, the option to cut across doesn't even come up. Clinging to shore saddles us with a half day's extra paddling, but the ghosts of last year's canoeists hover over the gaping stretch of water palpably enough to silence any thought of striking out for the distant point.

It is along the far shoreline of Button Bay that the ocean swell comes up. The waves are gray, lumpy masses, broad as hills. The canoes ride up and over them smoothly and then disappear from sight in the troughs. The motion is sedate, measured, and menacing. The wind is barely a whisper, but the waves are there, responding to some force out of our comprehension, power beyond measure. A seal rises nearby, floats on its back, and watches us pass with liquid, questioning eyes.

Where we turn the canoes in for the day, the rocky shore rises steeply out of the water. Breakers crash against ridges of cobbles. Like surfers, we try to catch a final wave and ride the crest in. As each boat strikes shore, the bow person vaults out. The stern people are drenched by the next breaking wave before they can scramble over the load.

Camp is almost in the shadow of Fort Prince of Wales. Churchill is around the point and across the wide mouth of the Churchill River. The fort is a squat stone monolith that took the British more than forty years to construct, starting in 1731, and was then surrendered to the French without a cannon being fired in 1782. It is bunker-like, primitive in appearance in the way armored boats from the Civil War look primitive—a structure with enough weight to make the crust of the earth dip down, ever so slightly.

This point has a steep shoreline and deep water, which is why Churchill is a port for shipping grain north by train from the heartland prairie provinces of Canada. The shipping season is an agonizingly short couple of months. Some years the first boat can't get through the ice until August.

If the land keeps rebounding, in a few millennia Churchill will be an inland town full of coastal artifacts. The tundra will creep slowly forward to colonize what is now the ocean's domain. The Churchill River will have to carve a canyon if it is to keep its channel. Hudson Bay, in fact, will disappear altogether; its average depth now is only 330 feet. In twenty thousand years Fort Prince of Wales may rise to a commanding 1,500 feet above sea level, perched outlandishly on the brink of the Churchill River gorge.

Who knows? A lot could happen, given enough time.

On the final morning there are strange sounds in the air: deep grunts and rumbles, snatches of eerie song coming from the sea. Belugas. The small, white whales are off the point, cruising nearby, rising to blow, talking. A pod of six or eight is thrashing around in the water when we start to paddle, and we stroke toward them.

They are oblivious to us. Something is going on. The group of sleek whales is lathering the water, their arched backs carving into the air, flukes rising clear. Mating, playing, courting, feeding, something. Suddenly we are in their midst and have to backpaddle to avoid a collision. Even then it is some time before the whales sense us and disappear beneath the healing surface.

It is only the beginning. There are hundreds, maybe thousands, of belugas in the bay, collected at the mouth of the river. We give chase when we see a nearby pod, but it becomes clear that the whales are as curious as we are. So we sit still and let them come to us.

Pod after pod cruises closely past. We hear the whales' abrupt, softly explosive breathing. Some of their backs are nicked and scarred. The young calves are the size of porpoises, gray as undried pottery, and even the white adults aren't as long as our canoes. Several times they swim under our boats, ghostly submarine shapes with strange blunt heads. Once I feel their sonar singing against the hull, defining me.

I have no idea how long we sit with whales all around, receiving this gift on the calm sea. Hours, certainly, but we aren't timing this. At some point it occurs to me that it is the color white that has informed these days—the white of polar bear fur, the white of beluga hide, and the white of the Ice Age, weighing down the earth.

Finding a Way

A̲T THE ENTRANCE to the
Community Center in Fort McPherson, Northwest Territories, we take off our shoes and set them on the floor next to an assortment of mud-caked black rubber boots, the ubiquitous northern footwear. I carry a batch of neatly folded topographic maps, 1:250,000 scale, in a plastic bag. We are here in search of advice. One of the town elders, Johnnie Charlie, has been suggested by locals.

We have already come some three thousand miles—crammed thigh to thigh in an oil-swilling Chevrolet Suburban ornamented with three canoes stacked pyramid style over our heads on a crude roof rack—across the width of Canada on a path roughly paralleling the Rocky Mountain cordillera. It is that continent-spanning ridge we are now proposing to cross at a low pass in the Richardson Mountains—only a stone's throw, geographically speaking, from the Arctic coastline where the mountains finally die away into the ice-packed sea. But it is thousands of miles and nearly a week of driving, the last two days on the Dempster

Highway, a dirt ribbon punched improbably north over the Arctic Circle to the oil fields along the Mackenzie River delta and, tangentially, to the few small communities along the way, like Fort McPherson, Arctic Red River, and Inuvik.

The Suburban is parked in a muddy field overlooking the Peel River next to the Hudson's Bay Store. The canoes are lined up on a sandbar, loaded with packs, paddles angled up in the air waiting for our hands to curl around them and stab them into the sediment-clogged, turgid current for the first time.

Northern trips have become an addiction. Marypat is finishing her college degree and sewing for a backpack manufacturer. I'm struggling to get up the first step of a freelance writing career and working at jobs as varied as shooing cattle into pens at the local livestock yard and clerking at an outdoor equipment retailer on Main Street. Our jobs are means to ends, one of which is to get north in boats every summer.

Each year's occupation is the hunt for another exhilarating route, new country to discover in spots that won't founder the bank account. Every winter is spent crawling around on maps spread across the living room floor, trying to coax country out of flat sheets of paper.

I stumbled on this route in the literature of the Canadian fur trade era. The idea of retracing history is appealing. The fact that a road penetrates this far north, granting access that bypasses the expense of a fly-in, makes such a trip financially possible. When we find the old Suburban for sale, it clinches the plan. The six of us—Marypat and me; Craig and his partner, Beth; and Lynn and Kate—split the cost and agree to sell the car when we get back. This journey is our farthest north by a thousand miles, our first trip to land where the summer sun only bounces off the horizon at midnight.

The advice we seek in Fort McPherson is simple: the best route through the Mackenzie-Peel delta to the Rat River. It is the Rat we will ascend, over the next two weeks, to McDougall Pass, but first we have to navigate a path through the watery maze of channels, pothole lakes, dead ends, winding river alleys, duck-filled ponds, and mosquito-thick air that is one of the largest freshwater deltas in the world. On our map the distinct channel that is the Rat River pouring down the flanks of the Richardson Mountains disperses into several minuscule, crooked blue squiggles that stitch through the watery thickets like seismograph lines with palsy.

Reports we've patched together from afar have been conflicting. There seem to be several routes, none particularly easy and one or two nightmarish. That song about poor old Charlie stuck in the subways of Boston keeps humming annoyingly in the mental background.

Johnnie Charlie rises as we enter the bare-walled conference room, which is taken up with a large table and a set of chairs. He shakes hands with each of us. He is a compact man with thick black hair and steady eyes. There is a physical poise and a quality of repose in his manner. He listens while we explain ourselves. We put the stack of maps on the table as if to start the real discussion, but he ignores them.

"Take the Husky Channel," he says simply. "When you come to a side stream where a canvas tent is set up on the far bank, turn in there. That's where you start against the current. Stay with the main channel. Keep going upstream."

"What about these other forks?" I push a map farther onto the table and point to some junctions that look, on paper, like places where we could easily lose our way. Johnnie Charlie glances at the map, but he is simply being polite. He is as familiar with the delta as we are with our hometown

streets, and his landmarks have nothing to do with topographic symbols.

"There's a tent and a fish-drying rack at the beginning of
the Husky Channel, but go right by that." He makes a
straight-ahead gesture with his dark brown hand. "At the
next tent, turn in. No problems."

WE ARE NOT THE FIRST to be lured north by the gun-
sight notch in these Arctic mountains. Nor are we anything
like the most daring or desperate or ill-prepared. Ours is a
recreational adventure, a summer jaunt compared with the
journeys of those who have attempted the crossing over the
centuries before us.

McDougall Pass is one of those remote strategic spots at
which geography, human ambition, and drama coalesce at a
single point. It is the lowest gap in the Canadian Rockies,
and it sits astride the watershed divide between the Mackenzie and Yukon River drainages. If that doesn't push the thrill
buttons for those of us at the threshold of the twenty-first
century, think what it might have meant one or two hundred
years ago.

While the United States was still in its infancy as a nation
and still largely unsettled, voyageurs and fur-trading compa-
nies had already carved up the northern wilderness in a
competitive frenzy fueled by greed for beaver pelts. Fresh,
virgin country, a shorter route, any geographic advantage
meant as much to the Hudson's Bay Company or the North
West Company as does the next generation of software to
today's computer juggernauts. This shortcut through the
mountains, a link connecting the Mackenzie and Athabasca
country to the riches of the Yukon, was a temptation impossible to resist, and damn the difficulty.

Then again, at the turn of the twentieth century, this corner of the world—Alaska and the Yukon—was flushed with gold fever and aswarm with the infected masses. Streams of the hopeful surged north, enduring any hardship, any indignity, in the rush. One of the most arduous of the routes to the goldfields originated in the Athabasca country of Alberta. Stampeders by the score followed crude tracks cut through swamp and bush and then loaded everything they could onto barges, rafts, scows, and assorted unlikely craft to descend the thousands of river miles down the Athabasca, Slave, and Mackenzie River systems.

If they didn't swamp or drown in one of the many rapids, capsize in a squall on Great Slave Lake, or freeze in a cruel, nine-month winter, the travel-weary survivors arrived at this juncture only to gird themselves for a final trying endurance test that would carry them over the pass to the fabled waters of the Yukon. There, they believed, at long last, they would make their fortunes.

ONCE WE'RE UNDER WAY, I catch myself avoiding the map despite my preoccupation with our location in the delta maze. The aerial view is too daunting to contemplate any more than is strictly necessary. The Husky Channel, one thread in the Peel River web, is the size of a respectable river in its own right. It loops ponderously through the low, water-laden landscape, which all seems to consist of varying degrees of mud. The river is only soupy, flowing land.

Within a day we come to the summer camp set on the bank of a tributary that Johnnie Charlie told us to look for. There is no one around. We turn in. The water is the same texture, the same swirl of flowing earth, on a diminished scale. Only now it leans against us, a force with the weight of gravity and the timeless patience of geology. What had presented itself as a novel immersion along the trails of

northern history, and a rigorous physical challenge we rose
to from the comfort of our living rooms half a year earlier,
immediately assumes a grueling reality.

The maps become superfluous. This channel of the Rat,
if, in fact, that is what we are following, is so winding and
tortuous that we lose track in the first mile. Our education
in mountain-climbing-by-water-route begins. The paddling
rhythm has a decided uphill feel, which will only get stronger
as the days pass. Our pace slows to the point that the spotted sandpipers probing mudflats can easily outrun us.

The current is barely perceptible to the eye, seen only in
the slight "V" of water flowing past a protruding branch, or
a leaf circling in a backwater eddy, but its resistance is con-
siderable. We are soon crossing and recrossing the channel to
take advantage of the relatively slack water on the insides of
curves. Sometimes a helpful eddy will power us forward and
upstream in a heady, but fleeting, moment, tangible as a tug
from a friend's hand. There are no more coasting respites
when we can lean back and watch the world pass. If we stop,
we lose ground, unless we are holding ourselves by an overhanging branch or are beached on land.

The delta world is dense as jungle, overhung with alders
and willows, humming with insect hordes, and stippled by
beaver slides and muskrat tracks and the stick-toed prints of
yellowlegs. There are, truly, few choices to be made. Tributaries marked on the map turn out to be tiny, mud-choked
crevices or dried-up trickles. Only once do we come to a fork
where we have to study the current and make some educat-
ed guesses.

As Johnnie Charlie said, there are no problems, other than
the thousands of strokes against the lean of river, the mud-
drowned thicket where we make a dreary camp, and the
anticipation of steepening slopes to come.

The demarcation between slow deltaic current and fast
mountain flow occurs in the space of fifty feet. The thick,

sluggish meander clears up, freshens dramatically, and cants toward the suddenly visible mountains. Mudflats turn to sandbars and gravel bars, and the river is chattering and vigorous.

We spend half a day at this boundary preparing mentally and cutting slender spruce poles, which we peel with pocket knives and polish by rubbing them with river stones. We are readying ourselves for the segments of current where poling against the river bottom will be the most efficient way to get ahead. Craig and Beth practice poling their yellow canoe alongshore near camp. It is Craig's first trip north since his dark, harrowing episode on Opacopa Lake. Lynn and Kate, who work the kinks out of their poling technique in the third canoe, hadn't met before we gathered in Montana to drive north.

Near this spot the gold rush stampeders also paused on a rocky river bar and took stock. The site was known as Destruction City, partly because it was the exact point at which many dreams were conclusively destroyed and partly because it was the place where all but the absolutely essential goods were jettisoned. It was, in many cases, the final straw, this obstructionist little river falling hard off the mountain slopes. Even after all the miles and obstacles overcome, all the fortitude and resourcefulness and endurance required to get here, this last challenge, and the heartbreaking view of distant peaks to cross, was, finally, too much.

The next morning my thoughts are often with the parties that kept going despite everything. We are prepared with the latest in outdoor equipment, are fresh and strong, and have plenty of time, and we are still stunned by the effort. The route we have saddled ourselves with, planned for, read about, and traveled thousands of miles to reach seems, at this confrontation with current, to have leapt out of the realm of hearty challenge and well into the frontier of paddling masochism.

Within three river bends it becomes clear that our footwear is the single most critical article in our arsenal of gear. We are literally walking upriver. For brief stints we can paddle or pole, and along accommodating riverbanks we ad lib a tracking technique whereby one person hauls the boat upstream by the bow line while the other fends the canoe hull from shore with a pole. At least half the time we are in the river, often in waist-deep water, battling rapids.

We start out wearing neoprene boots with flexible soles, which keep our feet relatively warm. However, they offer such meager protection that we might as well be walking barefoot across invisible terrain where every sharp rock, each slip into the cracks between boulders, every step on fist-sized cobbles is mapped by the bruises on our soles and scrapes on our ankles.

In rapids we lean on the canoes to take some of the weight off our feet. The lead person makes a lunge forward into a turbulent eddy or over a large boulder while the person at the rear tries to time the next surge accordingly. Often a good resting spot at the bow leaves the stern person in the full brunt of a rooster-tail wave or teetering precariously between boulders. The water is a numbing glacial melt. Between occasional falls and the spray of turbulence, we are wet to our armpits within minutes and stay drenched till we stop for the day, after only three miles.

The sun never sets: the days only heat up and cool off a bit. We could slog on endlessly in the Arctic summer air, but three miles is all we can do. In camp we hobble around on our bruised feet like arthritics. The next day we push ahead four miles, and by the end of it I'm wearing a pair of high-topped canvas sneakers without socks. Everyone is experimenting with foot wear. When I limp to a knoll that overlooks the valley, I can easily see where we camped the night before, one big loop down the braided streambed.

We are like huge, ungainly fish struggling upriver to spawn. We pause in narrow slivers of turbulent, aerated water eddying behind barely submerged rocks, like trout gathering for the next dash into the current. It comes to me how little I understand of the way a river flows, and how much can be learned through the bottoms of my feet. Most of the time we can't see the bottom. I drop into an armpit-deep hole on one step and then crash my knee against a high boulder on the next.

I come to recognize the dappled look of river as it cruises over a knee-deep shoal of pebbles, all sorted to size. I gauge depth by the subtle hues of pale green where the drop-off near shore is, the murky darkness of the deepest holes, and the frothed-milk lather in the fast shallows.

We climb over the contour lines on the map, real as rungs on a ladder, sometimes two hundred feet in a day. Scraggly spruces clothe the banks, reach tentatively up some wet tributaries, and then give way to tussocks and cotton grass rolling off in a green, spongy mass cut with caribou trails, marked with wolf and grizzly turds, and droning with mosquitoes. Beyond, the frost-riven peaks and ridges sawing across pale sky.

Somewhere in the first fast-water days we pass the overgrown ruins of the cabin of Albert Johnson, the notorious Mad Trapper of the Rat River. From all reports, and the reports are conflicting, Johnson was a misanthrope with a shiftless history and rumored links to a string of unsolved crimes, even a handful of murders. When the Royal Canadian Mounted Police came to visit Johnson just after Christmas in 1931, what started as a routine investigation over a trapping dispute escalated into a mid-winter manhunt when Johnson fired a shot through the cabin door and wounded one of the officers.

After the Mounties attempted a siege in minus-forty-degree darkness, Johnson made his escape and began an incredible solo crossing of the Richardson Mountains. The lone trapper endured consistent temperatures of forty and fifty degrees below zero, covering his tracks and creating diversions the entire way. When he crossed a creek, he found glare ice that would leave no mark. He stuck to windswept ridges that were free of snow, snared rabbits for food rather than risk a rifle shot, built tiny fires beneath snowbanks, and wore his snowshoes backwards.

Despite the advantages of radio communications, dog teams, and, later, air support, the Mounties were unable to capture Johnson. On January 30, 1932, thinking they'd trapped the fugitive in a narrow tributary canyon, they set up an ambush. But Johnson again held off the attack and, in the firefight, killed one of the officers. Then he escaped in darkness by climbing a vertical cliff of rock and ice, chopping handholds with his axe.

It wasn't until February 17, after nearly forty days on the run and a staggering feat of endurance, that Johnson was finally gunned down on the Eagle River, on the western side of the Richardsons. He was emaciated when he died. His actual route over the range was never ascertained, his motives have never been made clear, no relative has ever surfaced, and even his true identity remains uncertain.

Several times during our less spectacular ascent we take time to rest up and explore. The lower peaks are jumbled summits of talus painted with bright lichens and feathered with caribou trails. The views are of green space, horizons humming with silence, dry ridges snaking off, and below us, the verdant river valley we are beetling up.

The lowlands are made of ankle-twisting tussocks, fields of nodding cotton grass, and an infinite number of stagnant pools resting on permafrost. Mosquitoes cover our legs in solid mats and surround our heads in maddening clouds.

Marypat has an athlete's appetite for physical challenge. She is no less staggered by the effort than the rest of us, but she takes it on, finds her pace, and rises to it. On our days off from the river toil she is drawn to the peaks. Once she is on top, bathed in the view and buffeted by the winds, some kind of primal joy bubbles up and breaks loose in her laugh.

She craves the height, the space, the flow of air. As the mountains begin to gather us into their embrace, Marypat hugs back hard.

But it is the river that occupies us. Day on day the current rushes against our legs, rendering our feet into unfeeling blocks. My sneakers, ripped and torn, collect painful small rocks by the handful. We drive grayling ahead of us in the fast riffles, spook trout from their deep holes, and draw swarms of mosquitoes from the underbrush, attracted by the aura of our body heat. At night, on the succession of gravel bars we camp on, I feel the tingling push of water against my legs for hours after we've stopped.

Mile by mile the peaks loom more closely around us, the ridges winding almost to the river's edge. We pause at a broad field of snow and ice and find a grizzly track the size of a dinner plate on the crusted surface. We are making it. What began as brutal work has settled into a daily routine. Some of the original appeal of the journey asserts itself again, and the intense Arctic space surrounds us always.

Then there is a fork in the river. A small channel twists through a tight rock cleft and into willows beyond. We choose the larger, more open branch. A mile farther on, a valley-filling ice field confronts us. We stand in the milk green current, canoes tethered behind us, and pore over the worn maps.

Must have been that smaller fork, we conclude, and turn back down, riding the fast chop in an exhilarating descent. Inside the entrance to the smaller fork, in the coolness of a miniature canyon, visions of our predecessors on the Rat rise up again. The river makes a hard right bend over a ledge of bedrock with a tricky corkscrew wave. It is all we can do to scramble along the cliffy walls, with four of us stationed strategically, and haul each boat quickly through the turbulence. Even at that, one canoe swamps.

As we paddle on beneath steep mud banks overhung with willows, I conjure visions of the twenty-six-foot North canoes used by voyageurs for river travel and of the sturdy, taciturn, pipe-smoking men bumping the heavy craft over bedrock. Or of the disheveled, exhausted seekers of gold, with their clumsy scows and cobbled-together rafts, confronting one more obstacle in a course that must, by then, have seemed an endless purgatory.

After the ledge the river gradient flattens, as if we've stepped across a threshold. Now we can paddle and pole nonstop. A tawny wolf appears suddenly on the bank above us, studies us intently, and then melts away without a sound. The mud walls are so deep we can't make out the surroundings.

At one point the bank has collapsed and a wall of vegetation completely blocks the channel. The Rat simply emerges out of the screen of green. We have to chop and saw our way through ten feet of brush to reach the other side.

At a lunch stop someone takes a picture looking down at all of our feet. The lineup is a collage of abraded neoprene, toes poking out, shoes that hang together by threads and duct tape, and shapeless socks sagging around the tops of boots no amount of waterproofing will ever save. None of these shoes is destined for the trash. They are the single most eloquent summation of our ascent, our achievement.

It is late evening of the next day when we finally break into the open views again. The light is that protracted, glowing twilight that lingers for hours in the Arctic summer and then shades into pink dawn. The Rat is narrow enough here that we would have difficulty turning the canoes around.

Beaver dams cross the stream, constructed by beavers descended from survivors of the fur trade holocaust. We stand on the sticks and mud to scrape the canoes over. The little river winds in tight coils and loops; our view swings among purpling mountains and tundra so green it is almost black. On a muddy point there are wolf prints sunk an inch deep and a foot-long scat full of small bones and fur.

The plunk, plunk of our poles in the water and the thin splash of paddles are the only sounds on earth. The silence that envelops us, on the saddle of mountains at the top of the continent, feels deep and thick as a becalmed ocean.

When I look up next, we are on Ogilvie Lake, astride the pass we have inched toward for the two weeks since our meeting with Johnnie Charlie in Fort McPherson. Craig and Beth have already reached the center of the round, calm pond and have stopped. The water is utterly still. The light falls on them like mist. The mountains rise away, abrupt and monolithic, resistant and elemental, studded with fireweed and campion and lupine and caribou antler and goat track.

We are small beyond reckoning, alone beyond reckoning. Yet we have found our way, with threadbare sneakers and torn feet, with maps worried thin. With a visceral, bone-deep knowledge of this mountain river that we share with the ghosts of our predecessors. All of this we share, along with endless unsure steps, strokes, lunges, and hand-over-hand climbing of spruce poles, fading back through time.

Sandpiper's Story

WHERE WE SETTLE at McDougall Pass, flush with our accomplishment, there is only one place to camp—a rounded toe of gravel protruding from the base of a steep ridge on the shore of Long Lake. The rest of the shoreline is wet tundra resting on permafrost. We stake the tents in the hazy violet light that passes for Arctic midnight, still wearing our ragtag assortment of tattered footwear. Our plan is to indulge in several days of hiking in the dry mountain peaks that rise four and five thousand feet above the pass, a reward for the two-week uphill slog against the Rat.

It is only after the tents are pitched, the canoes are turned over, and the packs are stacked onshore, that we notice the agitated spotted sandpiper feigning a broken wing nearby. And it is only after a careful search that we find the four tiny, freckled eggs lying exposed to the cool air in a shallow scrape at the back of the gravel bar.

This is not the first nest we have camped near. More than once Arctic terns have harassed us relentlessly through an evening on a sandbar. Birds have scolded and dive-bombed us as we worked past their clutches of eggs on the river-banks. But this sandpiper is particularly upset and is stubbornly unwilling to return to the nest, even after we shift the tents away and take pains to avoid the area. The small bird flies in agitated arcs and hovers nearby but won't settle on the eggs. Later, after we've retired, I peek out the tent door and see the bird back on the nest, but the eggs have been unprotected for a long time.

Those four eggs are the culmination and promise of an immense effort, a continent-spanning yearly odyssey undertaken by a bird that is less than eight inches long from beak to tail. Four speckled eggs on a gravel bar on the northern rim of North America, a thread of life, the continuity of a gene pool, a grain in the sands of evolution.

We have come a long way ourselves, worked hard to get here. But listen. This could be, close enough, this bird's story.

THE SPOTTED SANDPIPER makes a short dash along the shoreline in the dark sand left by a receding wave. Air bubbles escape through small, wet holes in the sand. The bird stops to snatch up pieces of food, crustaceans or insects, and escapes a wave, running in front of the white froth to dry beach. He bobs several times and gives a sharp, two-note call.

The male shorebird, in his fourth year, has been feeding along the coast of the Yucatán Peninsula for days. Hummingbirds, other sandpipers, curlews, plovers, yellowlegs, and many other species clutter the shore. In the third week of April, new avian arrivals land each day. Others depart, setting wing across the 500-mile stretch of ocean to the north. Many birds, the sandpiper among them, wait, as if for an environmental signal, to set off.

As twilight shades toward night, the spotted sandpiper makes his last feeding forays and then takes to the air, heading toward the coast of Louisiana. A light breeze blows out of the northeast, and the sky is hazy enough to encircle the moon with a halo. The quivering bursts of wing beats that typify the bird's flight over short distances are replaced by a strong, steady stroke that propels it at forty and fifty miles an hour.

In the deepening night the sandpiper flies alone, aware of other birds around him. Strong fliers like plovers and curlews pass by. Even hummingbirds hurtle their tiny bodies past, their wings a blur of motion.

The healthy sandpiper flies well, feeling the bite of air against wing. The winter molt has furnished the bird with a new set of flight feathers, and his body plumage is shifting to the distinct spotted pattern of summer. Under favorable conditions the ocean crossing will take some twelve hours. For eight hours his flight continues methodically north. He feels only slight muscle fatigue.

During the next hour, however, the thin haze begins to thicken and spread across the night sky, obscuring the stars. The wind veers to the north and grows into a debilitating head wind. The bird's wing beats become increasingly labored; his flight speed is cut by a third.

The sandpiper struggles to gain altitude. He climbs several thousand feet, but the wind is as strong as ever. Each stroke is a painful punctuation in a steady ache. He loses height and works to economize his forward glide. There are more than a hundred miles of open ocean left to cross. His body is already feeding on itself for fuel.

After a time the sandpiper can make out the whitecapped waves on the gray sea beneath him. He strives to maintain altitude, but his muscles are desperately fatigued. He is driven lower yet until he can hear the hiss and froth of the lathered ocean.

Through the darkness there is a glimmer of light ahead, like a star, except closer. Instinctively, the bird aims for it. His flight is heavy and slow, so close to the water that he has to climb to escape the highest waves.

Suddenly he is very close to the strange bright light. The sandpiper flutters in confused circles around it, thrown off course, and then falls exhausted to the metal decking of an offshore drilling platform. Mechanical sounds thrum in the air; the deck vibrates under the frightened bird. He runs toward a large box and huddles on the lee side, out of the tormenting wind, and falls into a fitful, exhausted sleep.

For some time he rests, hidden by darkness in the protected corner, shifting from one leg to the other or ruffling his drying feathers. With the gray rise of dawn over a lumpy sea, the wind settles to a breeze. The weary bird is rested but depleted. When he hears human voices and increased activity, he flies up to a thin guy wire.

The sandpiper flies off again, toward the coast that lies only forty miles away, wing muscles burning. An hour later a huge red sun rises over the eastern waterline and illuminates a low, sandy island off the Louisiana coast. The spotted sandpiper shifts into a short glide, lands on the damp sand, and bobs twice.

Within minutes the bird is feeding in the mist. Once his hunger is assuaged, the shorebird turns to preening and looking about. Many other birds, survivors of the long crossing, crowd the small island. The spotted sandpiper bobs; makes a short, curving flight over the water; and then runs along the sand into concealing tufts of beach grass. There he sleeps again.

Over the next few weeks the sandpiper presses north against the retreating winter. In time his body recovers from the ordeal of the ocean crossing. The memory of his wintering ground at Lake Atitlán, nestled in tropical vegetation and rimmed by high volcanic peaks, fades away. The migration that began as a vague restlessness in the Central American highlands becomes more and more a compelling urge. The sandpiper pushes into the opening, greening, exhaling center of the continent.

His route follows river courses where he feeds along mud shores and small lakes. The sandpiper stays to himself, seeking safety in obscurity. Late storms detain him several times, once along the Red River and again on a lakeshore in southern Canada. Whipping winds sometimes make flight impossible and the shorebird huddles in sheltering vegetation.

He feeds less and flies more each day. The storms seem to relent more quickly in the face of warming, lengthening daylight and thawing winds.

One afternoon along the Athabasca River the sandpiper is looking for a likely feeding spot when the shadow of a stooping peregrine falcon crosses his path. The shorebird dodges once and dives desperately into the river. Just as he enters the water, the falcon's talons slice through his back feathers. The sandpiper swims away through the silty current. The bird of prey hovers for a moment, and then labors off.

By the third week in May the sandpiper is following the immense Mackenzie River. Spring has a tentative hold at this latitude, but daylight is almost constant and the bird's drive is compelling.

He passes over the Mackenzie delta. Unerringly, the sandpiper cuts across the morass of water to a small channel of the Rat River. Following the twisting river course, he leaves the delta and winds up into the rugged, thawing foothills.

On one of the endless Arctic days toward the end of May the sandpiper wings over McDougall Pass, on the border of the Northwest and Yukon Territories, and circles the series of lakes, still frozen but for their margins. He searches the lakeshores and mudflats.

At one of the larger lakes, tucked against the base of a

long ridge and encircled by tundra, the sandpiper glides to a small gravel delta. He bobs several times, calling, and makes short dashes around the gravel spit before stopping in a sunny spot to preen.

The journey has covered nearly 5,000 miles of North America over a six-week period. The bird waits, now, impatiently, in the Arctic spring for the culmination of his breeding impulse.

For most of the next week it rains. The tundra thaws under the warm drizzle. The sandpiper finds shelter in scrubby willows and grass at the back of his territory. He hears other birds arrive and establish territories across the sprouting highlands: Upland sandpipers on a flat bench away from water. A pair of mew gulls that nest in a short black spruce on the edge of the neighboring pond. Two common loons that claim the far end of the large lake and fill the twilight with their laughing calls and wing-beating displays. A group of whistling swans fly heavily, sedately, soundlessly over the pass, their outstretched bodies white stains against the pale blue wash of sky. Early flowers push out of the moss.

The sandpiper protects his territory. When a shorebird lands on his gravel spit he runs at the invader. The flush and bloom and sound of life only make the shorebird more agitated. He feeds distractedly, watching for the mate that must arrive. Dozens of times a day he takes flight over the lake, wings held stiffly down, beating in short, quivering bursts. As he flies, he calls out.

She lands on the edge of his territory in the second week of June. He is stalking insects and doesn't notice her at first. When he does, he mistakes her for a male and charges, neck feathers bristling. She flies a short distance away and lands. He recognizes her sex and calls softly, his head held low and forward, wings spread. She pays him no attention, but eventually she returns to his territory. They feed together along the shore in the cool twilight.

Over the next days the male sandpiper focuses his mating drive on the female. He displays frequently, wings spread, head low, walking stiffly toward her. She ignores him. His display peaks, and then, as if released from a trance, he resumes another activity.

In time the two birds collaborate in building their nest. It is primitive but set in a carefully chosen site—a spot toward the back of the gravel bar, near the willow and alder growth. The nest is little more than a scrape in the gravel. The birds bring grass, bits of tree bark, and sticks to line the shallow depression.

The male continues his courtship, but the female rebuffs him until the nest is almost complete. Then, finally, she responds. She begins to display in return. Their feathers fluff out almost grotesquely and they circle each other in a stiff walk, attention riveted. Then the spell breaks and the birds preen before returning to feed or work on the nest.

When they finally mate, the act is a strange and clumsy climax. The female turns submissively toward the male. He flutters above her in an awkward hover and quickly satisfies his mating drive. Over the course of a day the shorebirds mate several times, usually obscured in the shelter of low grass or scrubby willow growth.

For the female sandpiper this is already her second mate of the season. Soon after she lays her eggs, she will move on to mate with another male, tending only the final clutch of the spring. The male will be responsible for brooding the nest and protecting the precocial young once they hatch.

She lays the eggs in the quiet early morning hours. There are four of them, pointed oval in shape and an inch or so in length, covered with brown blotches that blend in with the rock and gravel beach. The male remains discreetly nearby, occasionally bringing food to his mate. Within hours of laying the fourth egg the female stands up, turns the eggs, and walks off the nest. She flies down the lakeshore and begins to feed, bobbing often.

The male approaches the nest from an established runway through the brush. He inspects the eggs and then settles over their warm surfaces, fluffing his feathers and becoming still. He seems not to notice the female feeding down the shore.

For weeks the shorebird remains subdued and attentive. When the weather is poor, the sandpiper fasts, protecting the eggs. Even during fair weather he leaves only for short feeding excursions, always using the obscure approach when returning. He turns the eggs regularly so that the embryos won't stick to a section of shell. The feathers on his breast grow thin from wear.

The Arctic summer advances. The hum of insects becomes constant, relieved only when the wind blows. In the late twilight wolves sometimes howl. One warm afternoon the sandpiper listens to a brown bear rooting through the moss on the hillside behind him, tearing up the ground in a grunting search for grubs. The loons at the far end of the lake incubate a pair of large brown eggs in a nest made of mud and sticks resting on the water against a floating log. The mew gulls now have a nestful of hungry young. The adult gulls periodically cruise the lakeshore, peering sharply around for potential food.

When the people arrive at the pass in the first week of July, the sandpiper recognizes the sound of human voices long before he sees the canoes. A pair of yellowlegs scold in the distance. After a time the sandpiper hears the odd splashing of paddles coming near.

For THREE DAYS we explore the trackless, treeless ridges and peaks. The mountains are surprisingly dry, the distances immense, the views staggering. From the peaks we can look back down the twisting river we ascended, one agonizing bend at a time. To the west the valleys we will descend into the Yukon are deep green incisions below abrupt bedrock walls. Graying ice fields hang stubbornly at the heads of small streams. The high ridges are all riven boulders and shaley talus, colonized, here and there, with clumps of fireweed, delicate blue forget-me-nots, and pink campion. Lichen as bright as paint clings to the rocks, patiently gnawing them to sand. I strain for a glimpse of the Arctic sea to the north, that dull, flat horizon where the continent dives away to seafloor.

For two days the sandpiper continues its distressed behavior. When we are present in camp, the bird leaves the nest, tries every artifice to lure us away, hangs at the edges of the gravel bar. Nothing we do calms the shorebird. Only when we sleep or when we are gone will the sandpiper resume his vigil.

On the final day all but one of our group again head into the mountains. There are times, on these collaborations, when the need for a break from the intense interaction becomes a craving. It is one of these times for Kate. She stays behind to read and catch up in her journal. She is a tall, angular woman from Maine, full of quiet humor and solid practicality.

Once the rest of us have departed, Kate settles herself against a pack, resting her notebook on her knee. It isn't until after lunch, the day still and hot, that she notices the sandpiper acting strangely. Much of the morning the bird has stayed on the eggs, flying off only when Kate gets up.

The sandpiper is back at the nest, but now it is standing,

straddling one of the eggs. Then the bird crouches slightly, clamps the egg between its sticklike legs, and struggles heavily into the air. Within twenty feet the egg slips away and falls, shattering, on the stony ground. Kate lets out a distressed cry.

The sandpiper is determined. He returns to the nest, again straddles an egg, and repeats his attempt to move to safer ground. The second egg slips and explodes near the first. Four times the spotted shorebird repeats his desperate, remarkable strategy. Four times the egg falls and breaks apart.

When we return to camp in the evening, the sandpiper is gone. Kate shows us the thin bits of shell, the dried stains of fluid, and the thimble-sized, half-formed birds baking on the rocks.

At twilight one of the mew gulls coasts warily overhead, one glistening, unblinking eye turned toward the carnage.

Solitary

W<small>E</small> ARE OUT, this time, to cross the continent in our canoe. It is the most ambitious journey ever for Marypat and me and our first expedition without companions. What had evolved into a pattern of yearly summer trips together, every one of which ended too soon, has grown into this scheme to dive into the Canadian wilds for an entire yearly cycle, to watch the seasons come and go, to get beyond the clutch of civilization. It is a quantum leap, a project that neither one of us would have pursued alone but which our partnership has made conceivable.

It wasn't our plan to go by ourselves, but no one we asked could see a way to make the leap clear of job, school, family, career, debt. We hoarded money for two years. The food dehydrator hummed nonstop for ten months. The stack of provisions took over our rental house. Now everything we own sits in a ten- by fourteen-foot storage shed. Our civilized life, at this juncture, is in a state of hibernation. We have already been on the water longer than on any previous trip, and we have more than a year yet to go.

We have stopped where a small skiff is pulled onto shore, deep in the bush of northern Alberta along the Athabasca

River. There is no sign of habitation. The nearest town is a seventy-mile boat ride upstream. The only neighbor, a lone trapper, is twenty miles distant. In the era of the Internet, the shrinking planet, and cellular phones, there are no roads in reach, no train tracks, no settlements, no power lines. In a spectacularly gregarious year a person might get to town three or four times.

November through April the river is ice choked and treacherous. April through June its flow is thick with mud, fed by glaciers and upstream tributaries and full of cotton-wood trees and flood detritus. Three or four months out of the year the Athabasca is a passable highway, but even then it is a gargantuan flow mined with rocks and whirling eddies, with a patient, unbearable weight behind it. Canyon-carving, bank-eroding, boulder-rolling weight.

We have paused because we are procrastinating against the pull of whitewater that is drawing us in, half a morning's paddle away. Eight miles downstream the big river settles into one hundred miles of canyon-lined turbulence, starting with the Grand Rapids, more falls than rapid. That white-water will be the first real challenge we face.

The small skiff, the color of gray mud, is fastened by half-inch nylon line to a stout poplar twenty yards from the river. Back against the trees, along the high-water line, a wood pallet keeps several red five-gallon gas drums, an extra outboard gas tank, and a coil of weathered rope off the ground.

Then we see the narrow trail angling directly up through the grass and into the dense forest. The path has been pounded free of vegetation, worn hard as brick, by the footsteps of a single human. Eroded by years of trips toting water buckets, groceries, fuel, dog food, leg-hold traps.

How would a person end up here? The question forms itself when I'm fifty feet up the sloping path.

Two-thirds of the way up the hill, dogs start barking. We hesitate and then push on, into the shaded coolness of trees where mosquitoes rise in greeting. One of the dogs howls at us from the top of its little house. The others lean at the ends of their chains, their summer fur tattered and patchy. One is a gangling young husky with pale blue eyes and long legs aching to run.

Hunkered at the far side of a clearing is a low, flat-roofed cabin. There is a fenced vegetable garden the size of a house lot full of potatoes, spinach, carrots, and chest-high pea plants. The overarching forest has an expectant, colonizing feel, as if it understands the temporary nature of this encroachment and is poised for repossession.

He emerges from the cabin, buttoning his shirt, when we are ten yards away: a gray man, lean and slightly stooped, with two days of beard on his face and eyeglasses askew. It is as if he has stepped into a glaring light. He looks at the ground, sideways, into the woods, anywhere but at us.

"Traveling the river?" he asks.

Before we can answer, he goes on. "I don't come out till noon, most days. The mosquitoes get behind my glasses and drive me crazy. All these years, and I hate 'em worse every summer." His voice, too, is averted, so soft I have to lean in to hear.

"Come in." He backs toward the door. "Have some tea."

It is a tiny space, a den. His bed, unmade, with a snow-mobile manual laid open on the rumpled blankets, takes up the far wall. A small table and two benches fill the center of the floor. Wood cookstove, makeshift sink, and counter line the wall below the only window. A thin closet built into a corner holds wool pants, a few shirts, and several jackets on hangers. A worn pair of long-tailed snowshoes hangs from a nail. There is a half-empty bottle of vodka perched on top of the closet.

The woodstove is stoked and the cabin is hot. "Boiling my clothes," he explains. He lifts the lid off a large kettle and stirs the soapy water with a worn branch of spruce.

"Quite a garden you have," Marypat says.

"I like my potatoes. Something to do in the summers. The summers get long here." He gazes out the window; he hasn't looked at us yet. "The potatoes are so good I sometimes eat them right out of the ground, like apples."

We sit across from each other at the table made of pine boards, drinking black tea from mugs. His hands are nervous, reaching for things and then retreating.

"You're the first I've seen all summer," he says.

We tell him we've been on the water a month already, that we're going all the way across Canada in two summers and plan to winter over somewhere on Lake Athabasca, along the northern fringe of Saskatchewan.

"Never do it," he says, flatly, and looks at me for the first time.

There is an air of resignation in the cabin, of half-finished projects, paths not taken, abbreviated prospects.

"That's what I should have done," he blurts out. "Should have gone up north and looked for mineral. Cripes, there's mineral everywhere up there. All you need is a rock book and a hammer."

"How long have you been here?" I ask.

"Seventeen years," he says, and his hands sweep invisible crumbs off the table. "I came late. I was already forty."

"What made you come?"

He stops still; his mobile hands reach for each other.

"It was easy," he says, almost in a whisper. "Pick a spot, file a claim, and set out. The lease is only fifteen dollars a year. You get more land than one man could ever trap. I've never even been to all of it."

"But what made you do it?" I persist.

He turns sideways on his bench, as if he's going to get up and leave.

"The hard part is sticking the first few years," he says to the wall. "Cripes!" He is remembering—you can see it in the lift of his head. The crush of wilderness; the oppression of work; the brute labor of clearing and building, finding your way across the territory with dogs and traps; the brittle cold; the empty, barren days of summer.

I see him, clear as in a snapshot, motoring up to the muddy bank almost two decades earlier, boat weighed down to the gunwales with supplies. I see him turn off the outboard and stand, looking uphill at the gloomy forest. A belch of exhaust wafts away, and the enormity of what he has done washes over him like a thing to drown in.

He is talking again. "After that it's like anything. It's what you do. The years pass. At some point you can't imagine doing anything else. How could I go back?" he chuckles at the preposterous thought.

He rises to stir his clothes. We sip the strong, cooling tea. We ask about the rapids below, the portage trail.

"I've had trouble with bears every time I go down there," he says.

Not once does he look at Marypat. When she asks a question he answers to me or to the window. What is he to do with a woman—a young, strong, vital, attractive woman—in his celibate space? It is a thing he has given up for life, the chance for love, the curve of a woman's hip next to him in bed, the inebriation of female companionship. Marypat, I think, is too close. Her presence, across the table, robs him of air.

He lists the things he won't ever get to—adding to his tiny space, building lean-to shelters along his trapping trails, fixing the snowmobile, getting propane lights. "I'm too old," he says. "I don't care the way I used to."

"What's your name?" Marypat asks.

"Doesn't matter," he says. Then, after a pause, softly, "Eugene." He puts out his hand for me to shake. His skin is surprisingly soft and smooth, his grip fleeting.

"I've been sick for the first time ever," he confesses. "Something in my guts." He points to a prescription bottle full of green-and-white capsules on the windowsill. "Had to make an extra trip to town to see a doctor this year. Waste of gas," he mutters.

I wonder how much he drinks, how much I'd drink if I lived here.

"The truth of it is that it drove me crazy," he says abruptly.

I don't know what he's talking about at first. Then I realize that he's answering my question.

"That's the whole of it." He is the most emphatic and animated he has been. "It drove me bloody crazy on the outside. The stupid jobs, the bosses. Work, work, work for someone else's gain and for a paycheck that just buys more food and a place to sleep at night. Ahgh!" His face is suffused with the frustration of those memories, the years of treadmilling and bleak horizons.

I'm after something loftier, some bit of existential pith, a revelation, but his declaration has the ring of simple truth. We all come to those points where we ache to drop it all and strike off after something free and solitary. Eugene actually ran with it, and he never turned back. I am tempted to ask about family, friends, relationships, home ground, the things that keep the rest of us nailed down, gritting our teeth, but staying with it. I don't ask. We have pushed him enough. We are the first visitors he's had all summer. It must feel like being stuck in a crowded elevator, with us filling up his space.

When we leave, Eugene doesn't come out. He says goodbye from behind his screen door. I feel his eyes on us, on Marypat particularly, as we move along the garden fence in our boating clothes, with our prying questions and ambitions he doesn't believe we can live up to, our rude energy from somewhere as foreign as Tibet.

The Bear

Eugene's matter-of-fact statement, less than a day earlier, about bear trouble at the portage should have been a portentous warning, but I'm not looking for trouble, and dark omens don't weigh on me in the portage camp on top of the steep, quarter-mile climb from the river. The sleek canoe, overturned in the grass at the edge of meadow, is as out of place as an ocean liner in the desert. I lean against it, jotting notes, while split pea soup simmers on the grill.

The river roars through the gorge below, but it is out of sight, the sound diminished. Except for the boat and the mound of paddling gear scattered around, we could be on a forest hike. Our tent is shaded by a large pine. A grove of poplars lines the edge of the clearing, upslope. A single large spruce grows in the center of the meadow.

The mile-and-a-half portage can wait. The rapids downstream can wait. We are a month into the wilderness and settled in at one of the prettiest camps yet; life can wait. No, that's wrong. Life is right here.

The night is cold, and when I climb from the tent at dawn, dew bends down the tips of grass spears, glitters in spiderwebs, drips from the petals of Indian paintbrush. I coax a flame from a hot ember left over from the evening fire. A pair of siskins chase each other around a branch of pine. Nuthatches call from the poplars. The coffee is strong and rich.

When we get around to portaging, we decide to take only the canoe and some loose gear on the first carry, to make sort of a scouting trip, leaving the tent up in the clearing and our packs stashed against the trunk of a pine. A portage this long will take a solid chunk of the day. We have fifty days' worth of food in our packs, all of our gear and clothing, and miscellaneous accessories. The load is probably 400 pounds, and it will require both of us making two or three trips to get it around the worst of the rapids.

I loop a life vest around my neck for padding against the center thwart and start out. As soon as we enter the bush, mosquitoes swarm around our heads, land on our unprotected hands and faces, and collect under the boat. All I can see of Marypat is her feet leading off in front of the bow. The trail contours along the edge of the chasm. The Grand Rapids crash below, screened from view by dense vegetation.

Sweat runs down my face. Deadfall and gullies cross the trail repeatedly. At one muddy washout we detour into the forest, where the seventeen-foot canoe is as cumbersome as a grand piano on a spiral staircase. The boat hops around on my shoulders when I jump gullies or step down off fallen trees and wrenches me off balance when I slip. On a steep descent we have to slide the canoe under overhanging brush through a fog of insects and follow, crouched over like monkeys.

We labor through more than a mile of this before breaking back out at the river's edge, a place of watery intensity. A light mist falls, rain from the rapid's concussion. Whole trees, their bark beaten off them, litter the high-water mark. Downstream the flow blends, without a break, into the Little Grand rapid, still a formidable challenge. Water along the shore laps and jostles against the rocks, milling around before the next rush forward.

I catch myself looking ahead, reading the options, already antsy for the whitewater. We leave the canoe onshore, next to the riotous river, and start back for the next load.

Along the trail, bear tracks and scat remind us to sing and whistle and talk inanely. We move logs and clear away dead brush as we go. We are still singing as we reach the campsite meadow, losing the mosquitoes in the hot sun. The tent is where we left it, with sleeping bags still laid out inside, but even from a distance I see there's something wrong, something changed. Something about the fire pit.

With the sudden somberness of a returning vacationer discovering that his home has been burgled, I crouch over the ashes. They are scooped up strangely, definitely not in the way we left them.

"Something's been here, Marypat."

Then I see that our packs are tipped over and spread around. "Is that how we left those packs?"

My sluggish acceptance is as much a denial that this could happen to us, out here, as the slow focus of comprehension. Our lunch pack is ripped open, the contents devoured. An ammo can containing camera gear has been flung aside. The bottom of a pack with some cheese inside has been chewed into: there are obvious tooth marks in the heavy pack cloth; a seam is ripped open; the fabric is still moist with saliva.

We straighten up and look at each other. "Damn, I can't believe it!"

Turning, I see the bear coming toward us, twenty-five feet away.

"Hey! Hey, bear! Ya! Whooha! Ya! Ya! Bear, hey!"

We scream and yell like banshees and clap our hands. Our voices are high and hoarse with fear, but the bear stops, takes a small hop away on its front legs, and holds its ground. I am trying to remember where the shotgun is. We included the gun in our gear for this single reason, and now I can't remember where it is. Marypat, still yelling, starts scrambling up the lower branches of a small pine. The gun, I keep thinking. The damn gun is in the tent!

Our tent is directly between us and the bear. Have to get the gun! The bear watches us—heavy black fur, cinnamon brown face, no noise, no movement, impassive brown eyes observing. I step forward. Marypat's shouts fade, as if a camera lens has zoomed in and cut out all but this confrontation. My eyes hold the bear's. I have no contingency plan, no idea what I'll do if the bear charges; I am intent only on the gun.

I visualize the weapon in the shelter and the movements I will need to make to reach it. Where did we leave the front-door zipper? Is it in the near corner, or will I have to reach across to the far side?

I keep moving, slowly advancing toward the gun, the animal. The bear hasn't moved once. When I reach the side of the tent, the bear is ten feet away. Our eyes lock in the calm center of a hurricane. I have an urge to reach out and touch the animal, the way I might offer my hand to an unfamiliar dog. I bend down and feel for the zipper. Not in the near corner. My fingers work up the track. Where is it? Halfway up the side I fumble onto the hanging key, yank it down, then feel inside for the open gun case. My eager hand finds the shotgun. I find a grip and slide the weapon into the sunlight.

Remember the steps. Safety off. Pump a round into the

chamber. The sounds are metallic and menacing, the action of the pump a movie-scene noise. I aim over the bear's head. BLAM! The gun kicks; the bear recoils as if hit and disappears downhill into the woods. Jacked up, I lever another round. BLAM! Leaves and twigs fly off the trees; the echo is a shock wave. BLAM!

Marypat is out of the tree. We move together, fumble for each other, the gun hot in my hands, our heads turning, turning. We are wishing we had a wall to back up against, a side we could leave unguarded.

"Okay, we have to try and get everything in one trip." I start piling things together. "We can't leave anything behind."

"One trip! We didn't take enough the first time. No way."

"We have to try." I move into the clearing. "Start organizing while I keep watch. Consolidate as best as you can."

I walk away from the pines and into the open, the gun loaded with slugs. I see clouds moving in, but the meadow is warm with sunlight. I circle and circle, listening, watching, and periodically shouting out, "Hey, bear! Hey, bear!" The scene is out of a corny western. I am protecting the homestead, waiting for the next attack, the unexpected ambush. We scared it off, I tell myself. It won't be back.

Marypat has the tent down and the sleeping bags stuffed. I hear her pulling gear from packs. "How's it coming?"

"Okay; I'm getting there."

I keep circling, watching the borders. Then I see the bear. Brown face, black body, at the edge of the poplars, forty yards away, studying our camp. Aiming into the woods, I fire. BLAM! The bear runs off, using the trees for cover, loping into the gully below our tent site. Marypat, having stopped to watch, goes back to packing.

We have to escape. If the bear demolishes our gear and eats all our food, it will be as bad as being mauled. We are a long way from any help; an extended series of rapids and canyons separates us from the next town downstream.

Marypat finally finishes. The load looks only marginally possible: three packs combined into two, sleeping bags strapped to the outsides, pots tied on, zippers and pockets straining. The heavy duffle is stuffed with the things that won't fit in the packs. We'll carry it between us. Somehow, we'll have to manage the two ammo cans full of camera gear and the shotgun. I picture the trail ahead and have my doubts, but we have no choice. Anything left behind will be ransacked. And I don't want to come back another time to challenge the bear's claim.

We stand by the pile, mentally figuring the load. Marypat rubs insect repellent on her hands and face and then takes the gun while I do the same.

"Al, there it is!"

The bear has crept up on our camp, using the single tree to hide behind, and again approaches from thirty feet. Marypat hands me the gun as the bear comes toward us. So quiet. Not once have we heard it. Even in a meadow, it can get so close.

For the first time I aim to kill. Head-on, I sight for the chest and fire a bit low to account for any rise in the bullet. BLAM! The slug plows into the dirt. The bear bunches up and whirls in one motion and sprints uphill with incredible speed. I shoot again, firing up the slope, knowing I'll miss.

"Goddammit! I missed it!" We both start picking up packs.

"I can't believe it keeps coming back!" Marypat looks like an overloaded Sherpa, a massive, shapeless mound with two stubby legs at the bottom. "Let's get out of here."

I hoist my pack, letting go of the gun for only a second. We each grab a handle of the duffle, ammo cans piled on top, and stagger away from the meadow, looking over our shoulders as we go.

We stumble under the ridiculous weight and have to walk abreast to manage the duffle. The vegetation is so thick that the bear could be on us without warning. Okay, just keep moving. Think about how long the trail is, how heavy the load is, how bad the bugs are, just don't think about the quiet bear. I look behind us and listen for noise in the brush. "Hey, bear!" We keep moving, stumbling over logs, stopping briefly when exhausted. On the short breaks we kill mosquitoes.

The washout gully requires a tremendous effort. As I fight up the slippery bank, I picture the bear behind us, the brown face above us. Pace yourself. Keep moving. Don't think. Just get to the end.

Without the breath to talk we toil on, pointing out obstacles or blurting out, "Gotta stop for a second." My spine feels compressed by the weight; my arms ache from the awkward duffle. I think about strapping the gun to my pack and freeing my hand. The bear won't follow us, I reassure myself. Those last shots really scared it. But I keep hold of the gun and check to see that the safety is on. The weapon seems invaluable.

My sweat stinks. Is it panic coming out my pores? "Let's keep moving, Marypat. Slow and steady. We're getting there." I recognize landmarks from near the end of the trail and some of my acrid fear subsides. We are more than a mile from the camp. A light rain begins to fall. I can't imagine the bear chasing us across the portage. "Almost there, MP. Almost there." Marypat is hunched over nearly double under her load.

The trail opens up onto the beach, the pounding river, and our canoe in the rocks. "We made it!" The rain starts falling harder. We drop the gear in a heap, cover it, and pull on rain suits to wait out the storm.

Exhausted and immensely relieved, we sit with our legs under the overturned canoe, the shotgun just in reach, facing the Athabasca River.

"I think we're okay." I begin absently cleaning the muddy waterline off the canoe with my finger. "We've come more than a mile from camp. The rain will be covering our scent. It seemed as if the bear was pretty convinced by the last shot. It really ran off fast."

Even as I talk, though, I keep looking back at the dark, silent woods, the end of the trail that is like a doorway into the forest. I don't like having my back to it, but changing positions would give the lie to my rationalizations. I see Marypat turning every few seconds, too. I keep cleaning dirt off the canoe with nervous energy.

"That bear sure must have liked those garlic biscuits." I manage a laugh. "It ate them plastic bag and all. Probably couldn't stand the thought of letting any more of them get away!"

Time passes. If the bear were going to follow us, it would be here by now. I look behind less frequently and start thinking about the rapids ahead. We relive the confrontation. "I've never seen a bear so persistent!" I see blue sky at the edge of the storm cloud. When the rain ends, we can pack up and leave this place behind.

"Al, there it is again!"

The fear in Marypat's voice is like an electric prod shocking me to my feet. I start moving around the boat to use it for cover. "I don't see it, Marypat! Where is it?" Marypat is scrabbling under the boat for the gun I've forgotten. She gets it out and backs toward me. "Right there," she says, pointing. I am looking into the woods, expecting to see the mute face in the screen of trees, but Marypat is pointing to the side, on the beach.

Christ, right there! The bear has run to the water's edge, ten feet away, and has its head swiveled toward us, scenting for information. Marypat tosses me the gun.

For the fourth time I raise the shotgun toward our tormentor. The bear's scenting face is turned my way. I don't think through the steps this time, and there is no longer any equivocation. Rain has wetted the bear's fur, so it looks smaller than before. My intensity of focus blots out the crescendo of river, the rain drizzling from the sky, everything but the bear. Instead of hearing the blast of the gun, I feel the solid kick and see a bloom of crimson burst out in the black fur just behind the bear's shoulder.

The bear whirls away, stumbling, and starts off at a run. I pump in another round, still concentrating terrifically, sight, and see another blotch appear on the bear's haunch. Still running into the driftwood, the bear disappears near a thicket of alders.

"Al. Stop! You hit it!" Marypat has backed away from the line of fire, her hands pulling nervously at her rain jacket.

The bear is gone again. Dead? Mortally wounded? I'm sure I made solid hits, but could the animal be alive and close by? I'm ready to believe anything. We retreat, backing up to the very end of a gravel spit, the river one step behind us. I reload and hold the hot gun, bitter with the smell of explosion, under my rain gear.

"Jesus. It followed us! Actually followed us all the way across!" I have a knot of tension in my back the size of a softball. "I think I killed it." My voice is quivering. "I hit right where I aimed. I saw blood where it hit." We keep watching the woods, the silent woods.

Marypat is shivering, her body hunched with strain, her eyes roving up and down the beach.

The rain slackens enough so I can take the shotgun from under my jacket. "We should look for blood. We have to know." I imagine the wounded animal at the edge of the alder, imagine coming upon it, the black lunging shape. We wait until the rain ends and the cloud moves off up the valley.

Ready to defend ourselves, we creep toward our last sight-ing. There is blood on a rock, a dark red spot, and then another. I edge toward the alders, gun up, safety off, a round in the chamber. At the same time, I'm ready to flee. I step to the top of a large, river-beaten tree trunk, slippery with rain, and look around.

There it is, twenty feet away.

Even at a distance I know the bear is dead. The black fur looks like a rug thrown down in the pile of wood, without shape, without energy. "I see it, Marypat. I think it's dead." Circling around, gun still aimed, ready for a surprise, the knot in my back clenched like a fist, I move in. I can see the eyes, like display eyes at a museum, glass eyes. A stream of blood flows out of the bear's mouth, shockingly red against the black body.

"Be careful, Al!" Marypat stands at a distance. I pick up a round rock and toss it. It hits the bear's chest with a hollow thunk. "It's dead. It's dead."

Only then do I realize that I'm shaking, shivering with the collapse of adrenaline, releasing the spring that had wound more and more tightly with each episode of the afternoon. My relief is so powerful I can almost smell it, but the very last thing I feel is triumph. The dead bear lying in the rocks is a sad thing, an ending I don't want to own. I notice the small details—the thickly padded paws, heavy claws, yellowed teeth, and bloody chest wound, the way a stick of driftwood pokes up under the slack fur. When Marypat proposes taking a picture, I am repulsed.

Curiously, I'm tempted to unhook the bear's hide from the stick, as if to relieve some discomfort.

Wintering Over

Marypat and I committed ourselves to experiencing a northern winter in the wilds on little more than a whim. We were drawn to the idea of experiencing the full cycle of seasons with the same naive energy that had drawn us to ascend the Rat River years earlier. Why not spend a winter out, in the tradition of early explorers?

Our romantic assumption was that something would work out, that we would arrive at the eastern end of Lake Athabasca, nearly sixty degrees north, with a thousand miles of Alberta and Saskatchewan in our canoe wake, and finesse our winter quarters. We'd refurbish an old trapper's cabin, in spite of the fact that we had no tools or carpentry supplies. We'd exchange work for rent in one of the small communities. Never mind the minor inconvenience of deportation if we got caught working illegally. Something would fall into place.

Our faith was stupendous. As we paddled the final miles of the summer, the reality of the challenge, and our complete lack of preparation to meet it, loomed larger with every stroke. But our luck was more stupendous yet.

One of the first stops we made near the eastern end of Lake Athabasca was at an isolated fishing camp set deep inside Otherside Bay. Within hours of our meeting the camp owners, they were pressing us to stay on for the winter as informal caretakers, offering the leftover food from the summer, a mobile phone charged by car battery, and the use of a small, winterized cabin that we would help build over the next month. The offer came so suddenly, the solution to our problems fell into our laps so effortlessly, that we hesitated for several days before accepting.

From the end of September, when the fishing season waned, to the following June, when the ice finally broke up on the big lake, we lived at the back of the quiet northern bay where the Otherside River pours in through a fringe of jack pines and poplars. Through the sunless hours that lasted from three in the afternoon to almost eleven the next morning at winter's lowest ebb, we listened to trees popping in minus-forty-degree darkness, to ice booming and singing on the open lake, to wolves greeting the crystalline night.

We pounded our water hole free of ice every day, cut wood by hand to warm our den, made trails through the boreal expanse, came to know the wild things that were, in a completely real way, our neighbors—snowshoe hares, willow ptarmigans, lynxes, silver foxes, spruce grouse, boreal chickadees, wolves, river otters. Night after night we watched, from the frozen stage of bay ice, the ephemeral play of northern lights wreathing the star-pricked blackness.

Except for the otherworldly news we listened to on a battery-operated radio, and rare visits from townspeople on snowmobiles, the months were expanses of muffled quiet, hunkered patience, unrelieved beauty, and desperate confinement. Our canoe rested through the brittle cold in the dining room of the main lodge. Nine months between open water. Three-quarters of the northern year in the strait-jacket of a season.

A northern winter is an odyssey that, unless you live through one, is accessible only in a vague and cerebral way. And the strange truth is that even when you have just spent a winter out, the very idea of winter shifts to a dislocated and remote memory as soon as the fat spring sun returns, the birds flood back north, and the ice goes gray and thin and pitted.

For months at a stretch we felt marooned from civilization and our network of friends, but our experience was a pale shadow of the winters endured by people like Meriwether Lewis and William Clark, Alexander Mackenzie, George Back, and Leonidas Hubbard. For them, it was very much as if they had fallen off the edge of the earth. The society that cared about their fates—governments, business ventures, families—simply waited, as if peering into a vast chasm of silence, until they returned, or until they were absent so long that they were given up for dead.

Months or years later their stories would become known. Some returned in robust health, bursting with knowledge, with the look in their eyes of men who had seen and experienced things that the rest of humdrum society could only strain to imagine. Others straggled back, gaunt, scarred, and diminished by the brutality of their experience. A few more were swallowed up in the void.

For most it was not the danger of rapids or storms or appalling physical toil that crippled and broke them, or even the disappointment of failed expectations, but rather the months of darkness and cold and the seemingly endless stretches of inactivity and confinement.

Historically, summer has been the season of glory for explorers and adventurers who traveled by water. Summer was the time for discovery, the time when rivers could be charted, northern oceans sailed, passages found, new lands claimed and explored. Winter, on the other hand, was the bleak season, a dark time to endure, month after month of starvation, bickering, and scurvy: the price one paid for probing the far frontiers.

From our vantage, wintering over seems a distant and archaic necessity, practiced by Old World explorers or members of nineteenth century polar expeditions. But our memories are short. It is only in the past seventy years or so that airplane travel and communications technology have allowed the luxury of summer exploration without paying winter's price. And today even those of us who choose to take up that seasonal challenge have access to radio communication, emergency beacons that beep into satellite-infested skies, and rescue by air.

Take the Lewis and Clark expedition, that legendary Voyage of Destiny. We all know of their slog up the Missouri River and their portage over the Rocky Mountains, but we tend to gloss over the fact that the thirty-three-member expedition also spent two long winters on the trail. The winter of 1804–1805 found them holed up in Mandan country, in present-day North Dakota, where their greatest difficulty seems to have arisen from the challenges of negotiating peace among surrounding Indian tribes. Nevertheless, the trials of minus-forty-degree cold, an uneven supply of food, and months of inactivity prompted them to depart before the end of March.

Their second winter, spent at the mouth of the Columbia River, was a miserable affair. They arrived at the ocean in November only to be hammered by weeks of storm. One November journal entry reads, "All our baggage, as well as ourselves, were thoroughly wet with the rain, which did not cease during the day; it continued violently during the night, in the course of which the tide reached the logs on which we lay, and set them afloat."

Not until mid-December, after a month of unremitting rain, did they locate a wintering site and begin building Fort Clatsop. Of the dismal weather they wrote: "As usual it rained all night, and continued without intermission during the day." Game was scarce, and what meat they got quickly spoiled. Relations with the natives were often tense. Over the months men became sickly. They ran out of salt and had to start up a "salt-works" on the ocean shore. By March Lewis and Clark's men, desperate to leave, began back up the Columbia River in leaky canoes, weeks ahead of schedule.

Farther north, the winter season requires even higher standards of fortitude and endurance. Wilderness travelers either had to complete their journey and return to safety in a single, short summer or spend the winter in the field as best they could.

Where today we can arrange our return to civilization by Twin Otter airplane, train, or car, men like J. B. Tyrrell and Alexander Mackenzie had to scurry for home before the unbending seasonal deadline. Afoot or afloat, the race against winter was commonly the most trying and dangerous obstacle they faced.

The most harrowing part of Tyrrell's barren-ground exploration of the Dubawnt and Thelon River country in northeastern Canada came at the end, when he had to travel 400 miles of Hudson Bay shoreline in order to reach the safety of Churchill. Autumn storms battered the expedition. The men were starving, and their clothes were reduced to rags by the time they staggered into town.

Mackenzie, in 1789, paddled from Fort Chipewyan on Lake Athabasca to the Arctic Ocean at the mouth of the Mackenzie River—and back—in a single 102-day marathon push. Winter had already settled on the land by the time he returned.

Another northern explorer, Christian Leden, a Norwegian anthropologist who spent three years (1913–1916) among the natives along the Hudson Bay coast, nearly ended his sojourn at the start by underestimating the harshness of winter. Frustrated at being stuck in Churchill, Leden cajoled and bullied a group of reluctant Inuit into taking him north along the coast in an open boat. They didn't depart until September 30. After any number of narrow escapes, they were conclusively shipwrecked on the shoals on October 11.

On that day Leden wrote, "In sodden garments we are fighting for our lives with the strength of despair. In blizzard and darkness, and burdened with chests of furs, we painfully seek a way over rock-strewn shallows through surf and spray from the wreck to a bleak and forbidding shore."

It was only by virtue of the skills and resourcefulness of his Inuit companions that Leden returned overland to safety and lived to complete his project.

The 1903 canoe journey of Leonidas Hubbard and Dillon Wallace into the wilds of Labrador also tested the margins of the summer season, with the tragic result that Hubbard perished, a victim of starvation and exposure, in a lonely camp covered with late October snows.

"About twenty yards away I turned for a last look at the tent," Wallace wrote of that dramatic parting when he went on to get help. "Hubbard evidently had immediately laid down; for he was not to be seen. All I saw was the little peak of balloon silk that had been our home for so many weeks, the fire blazing between it and the big rock, the kettle of water by the fire, and the white moss and the dripping wet fir trees all about."

Many expeditions planned from the start to spend the

winter out on the land. Parties that sailed off to unlock the
riddle of the Northwest Passage, for instance, routinely
expected to be on their own for at least two years, and they
sometimes took enough provisions to see them through four
or five.

In 1829 John Ross's second expedition into the labyrinth
of the Northwest Passage enjoyed one of the most ice-free
summers on record. ("But for one iceberg . . . we might
have imagined ourselves in the summer seas of England," he
wrote.) On an eighty-five-ton steam packet and a sixteen-
ton tender, Ross and his skeleton crew of twenty-three
crossed Baffin Bay in nine days. Two years earlier it had
taken rival explorer William Edward Parry two months. By
the end of September Ross was plying unknown waters, having traveled 300 miles farther than Parry had.

Then the Arctic seas came alive, lashing Ross and his crew
for weeks. Finally, amid roguish icebergs and heavy seas,
Ross gave up and settled in for the winter at a bay he named
Felix Harbor. Little did Ross suspect he had chosen a harbor that was, by its shallowness and lack of tide, a prison
from which he and his party would not escape for four years.

For three solid winters the clutch of men waited for their
next chance. For three short summers they were denied
their escape. Even when the bay was free of ice, as it was on
July 24, 1830, the harbor was too shallow and the tides too
low to move the boats more than a few miles.

Ross wrote that "the sight of ice was a plague, a vexation,
a torment, an evil, a matter of despair." The crew's morale
sank to a level of near mutiny and open fighting. Boredom
was a crushing weight. Men "dozed away their time in the
waking stupefication which such a state of things produced,"
Ross wrote.

In April 1832, after three winters, Ross and his party
sledged 300 miles overland, hauling lifeboats full of provi-

sions, in a desperate search for open water in Lancaster Sound. There, they hoped, a whaling ship might find them. The men were weak and starving, the group's cohesion was broken, and the trek was a matter of brute survival. Worse still, they were confronted by solid ice in Lancaster Sound. There they endured a fourth Arctic winter, this time without the warmth and shelter of their ship, with the crew crammed together in a hovel of banked snow covered with canvas.

It wasn't until the following August that they escaped in small boats onto Lancaster Sound and were finally rescued by a whaling ship whose startled captain thought Ross's party had been dead for two years. Remarkably, only the ship's carpenter died during the ordeal.

Meantime, on the North American mainland, explorers often lived through winters in surprising comfort. Alexander Mackenzie, on his trip from Lake Athabasca to the Pacific, hardly made note of the winter he spent at the forks of the Smoky and Peace Rivers in 1792–1793. The season was a busy, industrious one during which Mackenzie trapped fur to send back to Fort Chipewyan before continuing on.

George Back, Samuel Hearne, Thomas Simpson, and many others routinely wintered over, or used the winter season to travel overland, as they unlocked the mysteries of northern geography or searched for lost parties such as members of the fabled Franklin expedition, whose 134 men vanished while searching for the Northwest Passage sometime around 1846. To them, winter was simply another rigor in a difficult, beautiful land.

Theirs was the model Marypat and I tried to emulate. We clung to a daily regimen of chores and exercise to stave off the infection of cabin fever. The food and supplies we had shipped north to the nearest Chipewyan town at the start of the trip sustained us. Sporadic visitors—bush pilots and locals on snowmobiles—broke the monotony and the weeks of isolation.

We were, to a remarkable degree, comfortable. Our existence had a stripped-down simplicity—no pipes to freeze, no jobs to get to, no errands to run, no car to start. If it was forty-five below with a ground blizzard howling, we stoked up the woodstove, put on another pot of coffee, and watched the spectacle.

Modern history also is not immune to examples of winter tragedy in the north. In 1926–1927 John Hornby set out across the tundra barrens in Canada's Northwest Territories to winter along the Thelon River with two companions, Harold Adlard and young Edgar Christian. It is easy to second-guess Hornby's apparent lack of preparation, but at the very least it's safe to say that he was flippant in his assumption that he and his companions could hunt for much of their provisions. As it turned out, game was shockingly scarce and the three of them wasted away in the lonely log shack at Hornby Point, slowly losing their strength and will as the bitter months crept by. First Hornby succumbed, then Adlard, and, finally, Christian, leaving his poignant diary to be found among the stove ashes a year and a half later.

In all this discussion we tend to ignore the native people who took winter as a matter of course, simply one season in the land that was their home. We ignore them partly because they left few accounts of their trials and triumphs. We ignore them, too, because they were so incredibly competent at surviving in lands that, from a distance, seem utterly uninhabitable.

Yet winter exacted its toll without regard to race or cultural competence. One has only to read *People of the Deer,* Farley Mowat's chronicle of the near extinction of the Ihalmiut people who lived on the Barren Lands northwest of Hudson Bay, to glimpse the hardships inflicted by lean years. One has only to see the stark black-and-white photographs taken by Richard Harrington during the starving year of 1950. Harrington recorded the fate of a band of Padleimiut who had been missed by the caribou migration that year and were perishing as a result. Gaunt faces peer at us out of tattered, oversized fur clothing. A hauntingly beautiful woman struggles in excruciating labor to bring a child into the unforgiving world. An old woman looks stoically at the photographer and is dead within a day.

These hardships are easily avoided by modern-day northern adventurers, for whom winter is the season spent in comfortable contemplation of the next summer's destinations, a season of map gazing, boat rigging, and reading.

Marypat and I could have stashed our canoe somewhere safe, flown south like the migrating birds, and returned in the spring to pick up our route again. If we had, the nine-month winter would have remained another blank spot on the map of our experience.

Instead, that season of climatic rage and soft beauty is a terrain fastened into our memory, awash with the eerie rivers of light running across black skies. Northern winter so fastened itself into our psyches, in fact, that five years later we were lured back to winter in the same sixteen- by twenty-foot log home at Otherside Bay on another crossing of the continent.

And even now, years later and living in town, I sometimes stop on a moonless night in the thick of winter and close my eyes. I feel the bite of cold against my face, the sting of air in my lungs, and listen for the moan of ice grinding into place on a vast lake that lies 1,500 miles to the north.

Rain

SINCE OUR FIRST YEARLONG journey Mary Pat and I have developed a decided bias in favor of solitary jaunts. What once felt daunting and lonely now feels lean and uncluttered, quiet and intimate. Our camp, this night, is on a narrow, sandy strip of beach backed by low, swampy land. I am back in northern Quebec for the first time since the Moisie trip a decade earlier. This time we are slipping down the other side of the divide, paddling north to Hudson Bay from the iron-mining outpost at Schefferville rather than south to the St. Lawrence. We are satisfying what has become an abiding yearning for tundra lands.

In the northern evening the sun is huge and red. It hangs, heating the sky with its fire, and finally flames through the uneven, spiky fringe of spruce. Even after it drops from sight, the horizon burns with color until we retire to the tent.

By morning, rain is falling, rain so light it sounds like dry sand hitting the nylon. The urge to snuggle farther into the bag is irresistible, until, eventually, the need to pee, the thought of morning coffee, and a niggling curiosity about the shape of the day combine to drive me out. It is my niche, on these one-canoe journeys, to be the first one up and to start the fire. The dawn interlude with a coffee cup and my thoughts is one of my sanctuaries in a day. Marypat covets her final hour in bed. On lazy mornings I'll bring her coffee to sip while she reads or writes in her journal.

Over these years together on bodies of water we have evolved habits and rituals of camp life as ingrained as decades-old household patterns. Before leaving the tent, I stuff my sleeping bag into a waterproof sack, roll up my sleeping pad, and pile everything near the door. We may end up staying here for the day if the weather turns worse, but it is easier to unpack for another night than it is to crawl back in and reorganize after breakfast.

The precipitation, more mist than rain, hardly warrants rain gear, but I pull it on carefully over my gritty shoes. Day three of a thirty-day trip is no time to get flippant about accumulating clamminess.

The horizon that burned bright the night before has disappeared, swallowed up in cloud; cloud that I work in, coaxing a fire from damp sticks. It is a place of gentle rain, warmer than expected, of muffling air that feels still and enfolding. Marypat unbends from the tent, works on her rain gear, peers out through the mist, and trudges through the sand toward the coffeepot warming on the grill.

The coffee is gone and we're cleaning up breakfast dishes before we discuss the weather. By then we've taken in whatever clues there are to work with, sniffed out the texture of the obscured day.

"What do you think?" I ask. We both know the topic.

"Right now it doesn't seem bad."

"Could get worse, of course. Then again, it might burn off before lunch."

Marypat turns in a half circle. "Not much of a place to spend time."

"I hate packing the tent up wet," I grumble. "But I can't see hanging out here for a little drizzle."

"Let's go, then, I guess."

The drill is one we could do blindfolded. Each piece of gear goes in its place; all the clothing, sleeping bags, and food are waterproofed; each pack is settled inside the canoe hull and lashed in. Lunch food, maps, bug dope, the spare paddle, and other odds and ends find their spots. The fabric decking goes on last, snapped to the side of the boat. Then we knock sand from our shoes, step in, and tighten the cockpit skirts around our waists. I arrange my jacket to lie outside the skirt so that rain won't drain inside. The only thing that is significantly damp is the tent.

It may be my imagination, or the perspective once we are on the water, but the drizzle seems more determined when we paddle off. No matter. Our gear is dry, and we are snug as ducks in our waterproofed boat. It is my day to be in the bow. The small river twists toward the short, gray horizon. Sounds are muted and hushed, and life seems bated, at rest, under the clouds. It is a nice day to be out, to be warm and dry in, ghosting through the miles. A day to let the thoughts drift and leave the mechanics of our steady, practiced motion to the nerve endings.

The reflective mood lasts for a time, but the clouds don't burn off, the rain does get more determined, and by the time we've been paddling a few hours, we aren't nearly as snug and comfortable. My hands are cold and slow, gripping the paddle like stiff talons. The paddling motion facilitates the trickle of water that slides off my hands, under the cuffs of my rain jacket, and on down toward my armpits. Under the onslaught of steady rain, and with the constant motion, even the best foul-weather gear gives way here and there—at a seam, for instance, where fabric rubs against the tops of my thighs. My clothes start to feel slightly damp, then wet in spots.

At one short rapid the river is so shallow that we have to get out and wade with the boat. Rather than soak our shoes and socks, we take the risk of going barefoot. Slowly, the two of us feel our way over the rough bottom, using the boat for balance and sliding over algae-covered rocks. At first the water feels warm, but it isn't long before I realize that my feet are numb. Near the bottom Marypat slips and yelps with pain.

Her ankle is bleeding where the sharp edge of a rock tore away a deep, inch-long strip of skin. Almost immediately the surrounding area turns white, then bruise-purple. By the time we fish out the first aid kit, dry and bandage her foot, and repack, we are both stuttering with cold.

Before paddling on, Marypat finds some snack food in the lunch sack and we gobble down fuel. A gusty wind drives the rain at us now, distinct pellets of water that smack into the river, leaving momentary craters, and throwing up small droplets. The water's surface is lathered with these impacts. The two of us bow our heads and stroke ahead hard to work up some heat. The smug confidence I began the day with has long since grown cold.

At a small lake crossing, choppy waves pile against us, splashing over the bow. Rain slants into my face, slides down the collar of my jacket, and strikes me with tiny, cold hammer strokes. I am not consciously thinking about my comfort and survival. Existence has narrowed down to negotiating the next rain-pitted wave coming at the bow, and the next; to making sure my lower hand on the paddle shaft doesn't get wet when I take a stroke; to isolating a wet spot on my knee and moving my leg to a new location under the skirt; to watching a gust of wind head our way, burring the surface of the lake. The world, everything that matters, is made up of these distinct events, and I encounter them with peculiar vividness, in slow-motion clarity, the way I've heard people describe the unfolding of a car crash.

"We should think about stopping!" I shout.

"I've been looking for a place for a while," Marypat agrees, "but it's pretty thick along here."

"We'll just have to make do, soon!"

I hate the idea of exposing our dry gear, crashing through wet brush, and setting up in a downpour. But I know the insidious tendrils of hypothermia and can feel them closing in already. If we don't find shelter, get a flame started, and warm up soon, we're in trouble.

"Let's try there." I wave my paddle at a small, rocky, tree-covered island ahead of us.

Marypat steers in against a rough bedrock shelf and holds onto a knob of rock while I stand up. I am already so stiff that I have to wait a minute and let the blood pump before I can step out. The lichen-covered granite is slimy, but three steps up and I reach a deep carpet of sphagnum moss. A screen of head-high willows soaks me on the way into a grove of spruce trees; my feet are squelching water in five strides. The site has to work. I can't accept a return to the canoe and more paddling in the rain while the wet and cold strengthen their hold.

There is an opening in the forest that is perhaps large enough for our tent, lumpy but possible. I mentally tie our cooking tarp between four nearby trees. There is enough dead wood around to attempt a fire and some birch for starter material.

"It'll do," I announce when I return. The boat is bumping in the waves, and Marypat's fingers, clutching the rock, are white. I tie off the boat so Marypat can let go, and then I wait while she unsnaps the decking, loosens the tie-down rope, and positions herself to heave out the first heavy pack.

It takes me five trips to empty the boat. I am drenched by the time I finish. On one pass, struggling with a seventy-pound pack, I fall hard on the rough rock. The fall is so sudden that I have no time even to put out a hand, but we hardly comment. I get up and keep going. Marypat collects the last things from the unsteady canoe. Then we haul the boat up, tie it to a clump of willow trunks, and turn it over for the day.

"Tent over there, fire tarp here," I point out the sites while Marypat assesses the gloomy thicket.

"I guess it will work," she says, and bends to unbuckle the tent from the side of a pack.

While she starts laying out the tent, I cover the packs with the cooking tarp, and then I go to help. Our hands are working at half speed. It feels as if my fingers are twice their normal size; I have to watch them to be sure they do their tasks. Despite the exertion of unpacking, I am shivering, and when I look at Marypat, I notice that her lips are purple. We hurry to get the waterproof fly over the reasonably dry tent, but it is already soaked from the morning rain, and it sticks together, clinging to the tent fabric. Guy ropes get tangled in the underbrush.

When it is finally done, we take the tarp and begin pitching it in the trees, one end high enough to stand under and the other about at our waists. The packs go at the low end. While Marypat starts ferrying sleeping bags and clothes to the tent, I set about preparing a fire.

I try not to think about the hot, yellow flames, the first warm mug of hot chocolate in my hands, the comfortable smell of smoke. At this point it is still a distant mirage, too distracting to fall prey to. I stuff a fistful of birch-bark curls into an inside pocket. Some of the larger spruce trees have protective canopies of branches that shelter clumps of fine dead twigs growing against the trunk. I gather a cache from several trees and wade back through the moss to the tarp. I ignore the temptation to rush the fire into existence and, instead, stash the starter fuel under a pack lid and grab the small saw.

"How's it coming?" Marypat calls from the tent. I imagine her pulling on dry clothes, sliding into her sleeping bag, making the space as cozy as possible. But I can hear chattering teeth through her words.

"Getting there," I say. "I've got some good starter stuff, but I need bigger wood first."

I noticed several spindly dead spruces when I was collecting bark, and I head for them now. Branches or driftwood lying on the ground will be soaked through. Dead standing wood is our only hope. I cut down two trees that are less than three inches thick and carry them back to camp, where I saw them up and pile the pieces in a stack near the back of the tarp.

With a hatchet I begin to split the tiny logs, hoping to get to the driest wood at the center. The moss is too springy to split wood on, so I make one more trip to the rocky shore for a flat stone. It is the most dangerous step, splitting this wood. My hands can barely hold the sticks steady, they are small targets, and I have to rein in my impatience. When I have a pile of dry splinters, small slices of center wood, I find the trowel and dig out a circle of sphagnum down to what passes for soil. The fire site is barely under the eave of the tarp.

My fingers are dead with cold. I watch them blunder with the birch bark and the pile of twigs, disembodied thick appendages that have nothing to do with me. They shape the pile loosely, with agonizing slowness. They add a few of the smallest spruce slivers to the top and pile more nearby. All the while rain is drumming on the tarp overhead, falling on the precious dry pile that I hover over.

I find matches in a waterproof double bag, but the simple knot is insurmountable. I rip it loose with my teeth. The tip of the first match breaks off when I try to strike it on my pant zipper. I place it on top of the pile—more kindling. The second one sparks once but won't light, and it goes into the pile as well.

The zipper isn't working, so I find a small pebble in the dirt. Its underside is dry, and the third match strikes well, bursting into flame, but my hand fumbles it against the wet moss and it abruptly goes out.

I don't allow myself to think about how long the pile of wood has been sitting exposed to the weather. I quiet myself, take two breaths, and then ready the fourth match. I strike it on the rock and cup it carefully all the way to the curl of birch, where it trembles. The flame is tiny. I turn the match and tip it down. The birch sizzles and pops but resists. The flame is on my fingertips. I ignore it; I can't feel it anyway. The birch takes, flaming suddenly; resin crackles as another piece catches on fire.

I drop the match and scooch closer on my knees, hands cupped around the spark of heat. It has to work. This time. Starting over is not an option. I breathe the smoke in like incense, willing the flames on through the birch, into the spruce twigs, and up toward the thicker slivers of heartwood, where it is transformed from something ephemeral and unsure into something solid and firm. A fire.

I know without looking that Marypat is watching from the tent, that she, too, is smelling the smoke and willing the flames to life.

Tides

THIRTY DAYS LATER and four degrees latitude farther north, I idly notice the way water licks over the top of a small, red boulder. It's morning, and I'm piling packs next to the canoe, organizing the load. The day is drizzly and gray, with an upriver wind, and I realize that this might be the first river trip ever that I feel ready to call an end to. Usually the finish is an occasion of mourning, but not this time.

Later, when the gear is stowed in the canoe, the same rock appears to be farther out of the water. I'm sure of it because there's a small dry circle at the top now. I glance at the boulder one last time from the stern seat as we push away from the muddy shore with our paddles. The dry circle has grown. An inch or two of rock is exposed. We are almost forty miles upstream of the point where the George River flows into Ungava Bay, near the barren tip of northern Quebec, but we are close enough to the ocean that the ebbing tide is pulling the river down.

In the years since our first continent-spanning trip across

Canada, Marypat and I have continued to head north every summer. Each winter we pick an expedition route, negotiate travel logistics, dry food, make inquiries, and study maps. Each summer we paddle the blue veins through another quadrant of the Far North—Saskatchewan, Ontario, Quebec.

By now my writing career has gathered some momentum. Marypat is still nibbling away at her college degree and working at various jobs. We augment our income by touring the lecture circuit of colleges, museums, and sports shows with slide programs about the North. Our adventures have started to feed our work. Our work leads us to more adventure. As vicious circles go, we could do worse. We have no health insurance, no retirement fund, but we count wealth by different measures.

The problem is that since our yearlong odyssey, we go north with expectations that are fatally flawed. The qualities of that long experience—the level of mental clarity we reached, the absolute comfort we felt on the trail, the sense of marriage to a span of landscape, the depth of immersion in an endeavor—can't be matched in a few summer weeks. In spite of ourselves, and in spite of the fresh beauty we find each year, we keep forging north in search of that elusive level of intimacy we gained over the many consecutive months spent in wilderness.

The places we explore are all lovely and exhilarating, but we are spoiled. There is, always, a disabling frustration, a strange and unnameable dissatisfaction that erodes our experience. It lurks in the shadows of our emotions. Worst of all, it sets up a conflict between the two of us that was never there before.

Clouds lift; the wind dies. Like a benison, the sun comes out. It has rained for twenty-six of the thirty-two days we've been paddling. On clear days the warm roll of tundra distances, the lonely bedrock foothills of the Torngat Mountains, and the waterfalls hanging down the valley walls are enough to constrict the chest with their beauty. But for every day of grandeur, we've endured a week of leaden, soggy monotony.

There are two or three big rapids downstream. At high tide, we've been told, they are easy runs, but at low ebb they are tricky, full of boulders and ledges. After the whitewater the channel widens dramatically, becoming equal parts ocean fiord and flowing river. The map shows a rim of black dots, the intertidal zone.

Near the river's mouth sits the unpronounceable outpost town of Kangiqsualujjuaq, formerly known as George River. It is that native community, serviced only by plane and ocean tanker, from which we will return home. We have no idea, yet, how we will travel or whether we'll find a way to get our canoe back south. If there is one thing we have learned, it is that these vagaries in a trip's logistics, nerve-wracking as they may be at times, have a way of working out to our benefit.

There are boulders the size of trailer homes in the day's first miles. The George is the third largest river, by volume, in Quebec, including the St. Lawrence. Our paddling days have been full of reminders of the George's power—the hard slap of a side-curling wave, the dizzying spin of an eddy, the fact that we can canter down thirty miles of watery flow and still have half the day to explore a nearby ridge of ancient granite. The river's weight and bulk are as unfathomable to me as the fact that the gravitational tug from a lunar body 239,000 miles distant is sucking the water away.

I want to beat the falling tide through the rapids. We have plenty of food and plenty of time, but I'm in a hurry. The weather has taken its toll on my fortitude. More than that, Marypat's and my interaction, these weeks, has been uncharacteristically fraught with tension. Wilderness time, almost always, is our best time. It is where we find our balance, where the pettiness falls away, where we retap the reservoir of our attraction and fumble back toward each other from wherever it is we've been.

On this trip we have been oddly at cross-purposes. The friction is nothing I can grasp, only a vague disharmony in our rhythms, a striving for different paces, trip ambitions that grate rather than mesh. Marypat is hungry for an approximation of our experience in the Barren Lands during the second summer of our long trip, when we traveled 800 miles without seeing a soul and only rarely saw any sign of people. On the George there have been occasional fishing camps, we have seen other paddlers, and the pace of the river is so fast that we've had to dawdle to draw out our time. Her frustration and, to be honest, my own make me want to get on with it. I sense Marypat trying to force something that won't materialize no matter what we do, and I turn stubborn and mulish in response.

Once, at the end of a portage around a ledge, with our colorful gear strewn around on the river-sculpted rock, a discussion over whether to walk to a nearby waterfall or keep on going escalated into a shouting match. With the river pounding next to us and the empty, wild land stretching away, a month into the bush and our teamwork the only way out, we stood screaming at each other about a side excursion. The outburst was as startling as a rampant cancer diagnosed during a routine checkup. Loneliness is not an emotion I associate with being in the wilderness, but lonely was the way I felt right then. Afterward, we didn't speak for hours and could hardly bring our eyes to meet.

The grumble of the first rapid wakes me from a hypnotic silence, a trance induced by the mantra of my strokes. We hardly need to interact to paddle flat water and often go for miles between words, communicating the subtle adjustments through some sensory network built up over the years of fluid history together. The sound of the rapid brings me to attention, picks up the pace of my heart. Every new rapid is like this, no matter how many I've run. And this one is changing every minute—new rocks exposed, waves built up or flattened out, channels closed off as the ocean bulge pulls away toward Europe, lapping across the Greenland coast on the way.

I know we should scout, but there is no good landing to be made. At least that's what I tell myself. It's a long run, impossible to view from one spot. Marypat stands up as we draw close. The cockpit skirt of fabric decking stretches up with her and she rests the blade of her wooden paddle against the gunwale while she studies the water.

"Looks like a good spot just right of center, next to the big rock." She points with her paddle. "After that, it seems pretty doable, but I can't really see from here. We can read it as we go, or we can stop and scout."

"Let's read and go," I say, without hesitation.

Marypat says nothing but communicates distrust in the shrug of her shoulders. She has picked up my anxious signals, and she resists my push, even if, given another day or a different companion, she might exude the same urgency. Today it is my role to play, and she resists it. That shrug of her shoulders says, "Okay, whatever you think, but if we screw up, we know whose fault it is."

I can almost feel the water draining off as we dive down the first smooth tongue between two boulders. It's as if we're squeaking through before a door slams shut. The rocks wear high-water marks that are already a foot or two above the current. Then we backpaddle hard, angling the boat so that we ferry across the current to miss a ledge. The event is on, our quiet conflict on hold. The rapid unfolds into a series of quick decisions, abrupt shifts, and grazed boulders. The canoe dodges through a rock garden, hits a slot over a ledge, rides out a train of standing waves. It is like skiing—turning around moguls, making quick hops down a narrow chute, flying down the smooth runout, and making a long, flourishing stop before looking back up.

I know, at the bottom, that we've been lucky. We made a clean run by feel, reading water on the fly, our strokes nailing down our intentions. It could as easily have gone badly. One misread, one miscue in our communication is all it would have taken.

The chemical gush of a good run through dangerous water, that hormonal elation, settles back down to something steady, a metabolic all-day lope. Miles slip past; the sun is a high, sharp warmth in the blue sky. By the time we reach the last rapid it is unclear what the tides are doing. We stop at the top, where Marypat suggests lunch. I feel the same pangs of hunger, but my drive to get past the last obstacle overwhelms them. I trot off along the river-worn bedrock to look it over.

The rapid is a thick jumble of exposed rock. Most of the river's flow is confined to a gnarly center section, with big waves and no clear channel. It is as if I'm looking over a skeleton, seeing the bones of a wasted body. There is something out of place about the bleached stone, something unnatural about the anemic river pulsing through it. I choose to ignore the strangeness. It isn't so much that I go against my better judgment; I simply don't let judgment have its say.

"Looks like the tide's out," Marypat says when she joins me on a high spot overlooking the river.

"I think we can run it," I respond.

"I think we should have lunch."

"Look." I point upstream. "We can line the boat over that shallow stuff and then sneak down past the bad stretch on the inside. Lower down it looks like we can get into the main channel and coast out."

"Isn't low tide supposed to be the worst time to run it?

What's the damn rush? Let's have lunch and see what happens."

"Who knows?" I can feel the momentum of my irrational insistence even as I deny it. "It could go lower yet. Or the tide will come in and make the water really conflicted. Or high tide will make for big hydraulics. How long might we have to wait? Let's get it done and eat at the bottom."

"God, Al, what's with you?"

"I want to get past it, that's all. I don't want to spend all day here waiting for it to get better. We can run this!"

I don't wait for Marypat to agree but head back toward the boat. When she takes her time following, I start lining the first stretch alone, jockeying the boat by its bow and stern lines, one in each hand.

It's clumsy from the start. The canoe snags on a rib of granite, pivoting almost broadside before I can push it free. I get wet to the knees jumping across a gap, trying to keep up with the boat. Marypat is shaking her head, half angry, half incredulous, when I rein in the canoe below the shallows. She looks at me hard, as if she's trying to see inside, to get at me.

I understand that I'm wielding a kind of tyranny, but I'm beyond reconsidering. Marypat settles into the bow with an air of resigned protest, and I shove off before there's time to negotiate.

This time there is none of our usual teamwork. I don't pay attention to Marypat's strokes but horse the canoe toward a series of small ledges that I think we can slip over. Marypat sees another route and starts to draw the bow toward midriver. I ignore her, as if I'm paddling alone. Nothing has been said.

"Al, get left!" Marypat is drawing again, turning the boat.

We're too close to adjust, I think. I'm clinging stubbornly to my route, fatalistic, obtuse, deaf. Between Marypat's desperate draw strokes and my reluctance to change course, we end up broadside.

"Goddammit, Al, what are you doing?"

We hit the first ledge sideways, catch against rock and tip heavily, and then crash down the first step.

"Shit! Shit! Shit! Shit!" Marypat spits out in time with her strokes. "Why won't you listen?"

The next ledge is barely a boat length ahead, and we've turned the canoe only half straight when we hit it, almost capsize, and drop over. Another ledge. The same treatment. I'm grinding my teeth, riding it out. Marypat stops swearing, stops paddling altogether, and sits in the bow with her arms crossed, her paddle laid across the gunwales.

Now I truly am paddling alone, steering heavily toward a final set of waves. Marypat is my prisoner, partner no more. At the bottom I turn into a cleft in the rock.

"What the fuck were you thinking?" Marypat picks up her paddle, slams it down, and spins in her seat to face me.

"I'm sorry."

"You're sorry? Jesus! Couldn't you listen? Couldn't you see what I was doing?"

"I know. I fucked up. I'm sorry."

"We could have lost everything. What's wrong with you?"

"I didn't think we had time to get where you were going. I thought there was more water going over the ledges. I just blew it."

"We shouldn't even have been out there. I don't know why I even got in the canoe!" She lets out a bellow of frustration, stomps up onto the rock, and walks some distance away.

I lie back against the stern plate, thinking what an asshole I am. The sky is so deep overhead that it seems to spiral away in clouds of dots. There is a faint breeze just above the water that feels somehow connected to the velocities of river and tide, as if I am a passenger on a vehicle of geologic scale and have just stuck my head out the window.

Marypat eats her lunch with a ferocity that makes her jaw muscles bunch in tight, angry cords. She ignores me, so I study the map, with its brim of black dots at the edge of blue. I notice that the canoe has worked loose and pull it up higher. A minute later it floats free again. The water inches up the face of rock.

"Tide's coming back in," I say.

The sound of the rapid seems to shift. More bass, less percussion. Bones being fleshed out. Tides here can climb as much as thirty-eight feet from lowest ebb to full high. I tie the bow line to my ankle so I won't have to pull the boat up every few minutes.

When the water creeps to the toes of our boots, we climb back into the canoe rather than move everything, and paddle on silently.

We are caught in an event of massive, incalculable scale— on a par with slipping tectonic plates and volcanic eruptions. Only here it happens routinely, twice a day. Our canoe is adrift on the swell of the tides. Breezes gust across the wave tops. The third largest river in Quebec, at the peak of its volume, is meeting the oceanic swell of inrushing water, driven by its intercontinental momentum.

The result is a meshing of fluid forces that raises a chaotic, three-foot chop. The canoe jerks around like a puppet on strings. It doesn't matter what we do with our paddles. The issue is no longer whether we can get ahead; I'd be happy if we could simply hold ourselves in place. But there is no pattern to the flow, no rhythm. The boat, suddenly, is a feral thing we can't communicate with.

I think that this violence will be like a thunderstorm, wild but quickly past. I angle the bow in toward land and we pull hard through the welter of water. The tide is still more out than in. The canoe grinds ashore on an extensive mudflat near a ridge of rock, and we start ferrying the gear across dark, ankle-deep glop that smells brackish and fecund, a scent from the Devonian period.

By the time we're through, we've moved everything up the whale-backed ridge to the height of a two-story house. The canoe looks like a boat set down after a hundred-year flood. The adventure has blunted our conflict, but Marypat isn't forgiving me yet. She takes her journal and wanders away to vent on the page. I gather driftwood and kindle a fire in a depression of rock and then start a pot of coffee while I watch the water rise.

Half of the time the rock slope I look down lies in cold, brackish twilight, worked at by salt and wave and river current, and half of the time it is exposed to the air, beaten by rain, rasped at by ice and forty-below cold, and bleached in the hot sunlight. This forty-foot rim, this frontier, is in the grip of constant, rapid, profound change. The weeds and flexible grasses we slogged past in the mud, lying limp and desiccated, are at once terrestrial and aquatic life-forms. When the tides slip out, the flats are probed by predatory sandpipers greedy for insects and tiny crustaceans. Crabs and shellfish hide in burrows, some in states of semihibernation, until the water returns. Fresh and salt, air and water, sunlight and darkness—twice a day, regular as breathing, a hopscotch between universes.

When the ashes of my brief fire are gray, the water is close enough that I can throw rocks in it. Marypat returns, looking refreshed, and we embrace.

"I'm sorry," I say again.

We are no closer to reconciling our differences, but we press against each other, rest our heads together, and agree to go on.

The water is smooth, at rest, and when I cup some up in my hand, it tastes slightly of salt. We paddle across the broad mouth of the cove where the old town site is located, a relic of the pre-airplane era. It has a deepwater harbor that is immune to the tides, but there is no terrain for a runway. The entire settlement has since moved downriver, to a new bay near an airstrip. There the low tide lays boats over on their sides and strands people for half a day at a time. When the oil tanker arrives with its load of fuel, it has to anchor miles away and replenish the storage tanks through an elaborate system of pipes and hoses.

When we stop to camp, it is twilight; we have paddled thirty-eight miles from the camp where I first noticed the water going down. The black flies rise out of the moss in frenzied clouds. A quick dinner is all we have the energy and stamina for.

At dawn the water is high, but my sense is that our time is limited. Kangiqsualujjuaq squats on a low rise of bedrock across two miles of rough, gray water. A combative wind snaps the hood of my wind jacket. I'm in the bow today. The waves are big and the water shallow. Large, round boulders mine the crossing, their tops revealed in wave troughs. The way the water washes over them makes it appear that it is the rocks that are moving, pods of them rising for air and disappearing again. Once the canoe is let down on one and held there, teetering, before lifting off again.

The last quarter mile of the journey is a sprint against ebbing water. The town's boat launch and beach lie at the foot of the dirt main street. Weathered buildings hunker on their foundations. It is early, and no one moves about. Several fishing boats are already heeled over, like bloated cattle resting on their sides. The water is rushing away. We dodge through muddy rocks in the deepest channels and flail with our paddles but are let down in the ooze one hundred yards from shore. The last of the high tide trickles lazily past, like an afterthought.

A Child's Cry

THERE IT IS. A child's cry. Unmistakable. A child in distress, lost, alone, desperate—as recognizable as a siren, even at a distance. Then silence. It stops us there, on the smooth beach where we are packing kayaks for the day. I straighten, look about, look at Marypat and then the others. The images that snap through my mind are of search parties, a tragic fall, frantic parents. It is that kind of sound.

The protected bay is placid. Steep headlands, thickly forested, rise up inland. There is a campground nearby but no sound of alarm, no commotion; it is a still summer dawn on the shore of Lake Superior, with a child's cry, out of nowhere, rending the air.

Marypat and I have settled on a new strategy to shake off the disturbing wilderness malaise that has plagued us on recent trips. This time we have signed on in the company of three other companions, old friends from my teaching era in Wisconsin. Grant organized the expedition, so we have been freed from much of the preparation, and it has the feel of a partnership reunion. Also, the sea kayaks are unfamiliar craft, so we slide back down the learning curve. The very first time either Marypat or I sat in the cockpit of a sea kayak was at the put-in, two days earlier. For our inaugural voyage we are going to cross the 450-mile Canadian coastline of the largest lake on earth.

The distress call pierces the air again, and then once more. Something terrible has happened, that much is certain. No other explanation is possible. That cry is so clear, so unequivocal. Each time we hear it we stop, think about responding in some way, and then keep packing. I want to deny trouble, and it is easy to deny in the calm first light, with tiny waves caressing the sand and our sleek boats bright on the shore. As long as the cries stop.

By the time we're ready, the voice has been silent a long time. We are subdued by the memory but gird ourselves for the day. Each of us slides into the hull of a boat as if we are putting on a pair of pants. We fuss with foot pegs and cameras and maps, fit the thick round elastic band of our skirts snugly over the cockpit combing, settle ourselves, push off into deeper water using our hands like tortoise flippers in the wet sand.

I am in one of the first boats to leave shore. I rest quietly in the bay, waiting for the others, relishing the moment of calm before the daylong cleaving through water, the hour-on-hour cadence while shoreline slides past, islands approach and fall away, winds rise or rain falls or fog settles like a shroud. I am still getting used to being enclosed by the shell of boat hull. There is that joy of sleekness I remember from paddling the C-2, balanced against the faint panic of entrapment.

Drifting there, I slip back to the previous afternoon and to our crossing of Thunder Bay. I was teamed up with Marypat in a fast tandem boat that felt stable and responsive on the waves. Thunder Bay was our first big open water. A fresh tailwind pushed us along.

A mile out, the waves were big enough to surf on, at first by accident and then intentionally. Each time we felt the lift of a wave under the stern, we blasted ahead, sprinting for the crest. When we caught it, the kayak zoomed off as if we'd shifted into overdrive, leaving the other boats a hundred feet back.

By the middle of the crossing the waves were big enough, scary enough, that we weren't trying to surf them anymore, just trying to get across the gulf of water. A sailboat screamed past, heeled over and making for the harbor at full speed. Two blank faces looked over at us.

Near the far point the waves rose steeply in the shallows and others slapped back against us, rebounding off the land. In the bow Marypat plunged armpit deep into the surf, the boat shuddering from the impacts. In a canoe any single one of these waves would have swamped us. Even in the kayak, the air between us had that charge of exhilaration and terror. When we rounded the hooked point and entered this bay, it was as if someone had flipped off the wind switch. The water lay placid and unruffled. The wind was a sound somewhere over our heads. The day was warm and pleasant and serene.

Now my paddle rests across the neoprene skirt and my hands idly brush bits of sand from the deck. I keep looking into the forest, listening. There is some vague movement across the way, at the edge of the water in thick underbrush. Several of us see it.

When the boats are gathered, we all paddle that way. No one says anything. The kayaks are gliding through the clear water, rock and sand visible beneath the hulls. It feels like flight when I can see the bottom this way, as if I have struck an impossible balance. This winged sensation is peculiar to kayaks, in which the double-bladed paddle and the hull you descend into, make you, somehow, birdlike.

There on the shore something is happening, something mysterious and obscure and intense that we can't make out. As the boats draw near, a gray, furred shape flashes away into the forest; it is nothing identifiable, only a furtive, predatory motion.

The first kayak is almost on the tiny fawn lying in the rocky shallows before we see it. The deer is still alive. Its blood stains the water in feathery clouds. There are puncture wounds in the neck, torn flesh. This infant animal still has spots on its side. It begins to struggle and convulse. Its soft brown eyes are wild and distant, rolling. The bony head pounds in the rocks, under the water as much as out of it; the legs kick and make running motions. Dying.

And there we are, hovering in our gaudy boats as if this were a crime scene, an event we want to flee from but find terribly compelling. It feels as if we've walked in on some family altercation where we have no business and where our presence somehow denies the possibility of dignity, allowing, instead, only ugliness and terror.

All of us start to back off at once, loosening the noose of our presence. We turn the boats, drop our rudders, and begin to stroke away toward the open lake. Behind us, in the shallows, the fawn is still feebly thrashing, but the sound quickly dies away.

Summer of Birds

I DON'T KNOW what I think of any of this. It has occurred to me that these events, these interactions, have been in some inscrutable way triggered by our vulnerable and distressed state as a couple. How that could be, how such a thing might even be communicated, I have no idea.

It's just that these intersections with wildlife are so unprecedented in our experience, and the only thing different about us is that our life together has felt, during this time, as if it hangs in the balance. Could we be telegraphing our need for help, our lack of direction, so clearly that distant species respond to us? That's crazy. Is it that our condition allows us to see and experience things that happen all the time but to which we are normally blind? I don't believe it.

Anyway, the first thing took place almost two weeks out, well along the mud-thick Smoky River, in northern Alberta. This is our second yearlong journey together, capping a decade of northern explorations. The preparations for even a trip of this magnitude have become ingrained. We will spend the winter in the same cabin on Lake Athabasca. Many of the challenges we faced on our first long sojourn have evaporated. The year spent drying food, finding a renter for our house, packing and repairing gear, sending winter supplies north, refining the route—all of it is routine, a to-do list we have been down before.

But it is unique for the fact that we are driven by a need for therapy, not for adventure. The unknowns, this trip, are interior ones, wilds of the heart, untracked dunes of the soul.

For three years we have tried to have a baby. Instead we have had miscarriages; we have succumbed to invasive medical tests—sperm counts, dye shot through fallopian tubes, fertility drugs. Nothing works, and there is no discernible problem. Marypat has become obsessed. She rides a monthly emotional roller-coaster. She is biologically, chemically, and hormonally tied to our failure. The future we had planned for, had declared ourselves ready for, has evaporated, leaving us awash in uncertainty, sadness, and frustration, devoid of vision.

This trip, more than an expression of adventurous passion, is a result of that malaise. It may seem strange for a couple in trouble to head off alone for a year in the wilderness. To us it makes perfect sense. Alone in the wilds is where we have our best chance. If anything is to pull us out of our decline, it is months on the water, a delving into life along these pulsing arteries. Here the rivers, and everything they bring us, are an infusion as real as medicine dripping from a bottle into a vein.

But on this sandbar, with the river rippling at dusk, we are only at the start of the fourteen-month therapy program. Nothing is certain, least of all in the terrain we inhabit together. We are cooking dinner over sticks of mud-coated driftwood deposited by this year's floods.

A small bird comes upstream above the river. If a bird in

flight can be said to stagger and falter, that is what this one is doing. I am reminded of marathon runners at the finish line, ready to drop. Then the bird veers toward our camp, flutters over, and lands on the edge of a low step in the sand.

It is a female American redstart, a small, exquisitely marked warbler. We approach quietly to within three feet of her. The bird's eyes are closed. She seems to be napping. Marypat snaps some pictures and we back away. It is ten minutes before the redstart moves again, and when she does, it is to fly over and perch on our overturned canoe. Then she disappears under the shelter of the hull.

"It's too late in the summer for her to be exhausted from migrating," I say.

"She must have been attacked by a falcon or something," Marypat guesses.

We are whispering the way people do when there's an invalid in the house. While we eat our meal, there are occasional muted sounds from under the canoe, fluttering wings, soft bumps. Mostly there is silence.

Twilight is a gray cloak by the time the redstart reappears. She swoops out, perches on top of one of our packs and preens for a moment, and then flies into the darkening forest, apparently recovered.

That night it rains hard. I wake to the sound of individual drops thwacking into the sand. Big hunks of mud from the steep bank across the river slap into the Smoky like calves from a dirt glacier. Between sleep and wakefulness, I slip back almost ten years to a desert trip with Marypat. It is our early time together, and we are exploring each other as much as the canyons.

We are searching for a route over a large, high mesa to the next valley east. There are no trails. Time after time we work up side canyons in hopes of finding an opening through the tiered sandstone to the top. Again and again we are thwarted by the concave curve of cross-bedded rock, by overhangs, by sheer, steep, unbroken cliff.

At the final possible break along the western side of the mesa we find a low, rounded buttress the shape of a wooden shoe that we are able to friction up. Then, along a leaf of dark red sandstone, a narrow ledge leads off across the smooth, angled face. We edge out, packs on our backs, teetering in space on a lip the width of our boots. Next we come to a narrow cleft that we can bridge our way up, spread-eagled against opposing walls. There is no longer any thought of retracing our steps.

Where we break out, the sandstone rises in steep but navigable layers, one above another. We almost run the final pitches, our shoes sticking to the gritty rock, the valley floor falling away, warm winds rushing up with us.

At the top, in the shade of a juniper as broad as a living room, we drop our packs, take off our clothes, and make love. It is a joyous, naked grappling: the warm skin of rock under us, white-throated swifts bombing through the updraft, half of Utah at our feet.

Then I am back in the black tent along the Smoky River. Marypat is breathing deeply, invisibly, two feet away. I have been ambushed by these visions from less troubled times lately.

Lightning cracks overhead like a whip, searing my eyes. How did we get here? It feels as if we spend all our time thrashing ahead blindly through a dense thicket, on parallel tracks but out of touch. Once in a while we bump into each other, unexpectedly face to face, and don't know what to say.

Early in our relationship, Marypat declared what amounted to two ultimatums. First, she didn't plan on ever getting married. Second, she was absolutely committed to having children. Fine, I said.

The marriage edict fell by the wayside during our first

winter in the north. During that long isolation we recognized how important our society of friends and family was. The network of humanity we were distanced from was the one and only thing we truly longed for. To celebrate our commitment with them was the easiest big decision we ever made together. Marypat ended up proposing to me, and we officiated our own ceremony within months of our return home.

Now it looks as if her second ultimatum might wither away as well.

A week later, and almost 200 miles along the Peace River, an upriver wind harasses us. Current and wind opposing each other raise a strange and unruly conflict on the surface of a river. The current pushes along with its unrelenting force while the winds shove back upstream. The battle piles up steep-sided, tricky waves where a canoe tends to twist and tip. The part of the boat in the river is held in the headlong, descending grasp; the hull above water is pushed back, buffeted by the hammering tunnel of air.

It is rare to be windbound on a river, but the Peace is a mile wide, its volume measured in tens of thousands of cubic feet per second, and the wind is an unrelenting gale. We are making our way across the flow to a grassy opening, where we will stop. I am kneeling in the bow, digging in till my elbows ache, throwing in a draw or pry stroke once in a while to help Marypat hold our angle. Her struggle to keep on course is communicated through the hull and up into my kneecaps.

"Al, look behind you!" Marypat shouts.

I stop paddling and twist around. There on the fabric decking that covers our gear stands a spotted sandpiper. It has landed on our island to take a rest. The boat starts to pitch and wallow, adrift in the waves and wind. The sandpiper has a hard time gripping the smooth fabric. It walks unsteadily, leaving wet, stick-toed tracks on the deck, and then flies off again. The tracks dry in the wind before I turn back around.

Several days farther downriver we approach Vermilion Falls, likely to be the only portage in our 1,000-mile summer. The actual falls are preceded by a mile or two of rough water known as The Chutes. If we have to portage the entire rapid, it will be a carry almost three miles long through mosquito-laden bush. If we can sneak past The Chutes, we might shorten the work to a quarter mile or less. It is a place where desire is likely to color our judgment.

We keep close to shore well upstream. The river is smooth and unruffled, quiet and placid. A slight tailwind holds back the sound of falling water, which we have been told can be heard as far as five miles upstream. The only thing out of the ordinary is that the river's horizon line drops away ahead of us, as if the river disappears off a table edge or runs into a force field and simply stops.

I have that queasy excitement in my belly. These unknowns in a trip are both the reasons why we go and the points we most dread. Now I hear the falls—a mile of river dropping over a jagged limestone lip, pounding down a big stair step on the way to the ocean. The sound is elemental, earth trembling, a simple and joyful bellow from the earth. It cinches up around my throat.

A raven swoops out directly in front of us, flies ahead a short distance, and lands in a pine. When we come close again, the black bird does the same thing, leading ahead. It is speaking to us, telling us to come on. I don't say anything to Marypat. It's too strange. But I know this: the raven is taking us to a good landing. Four times the bird coasts off a perch as we come near, glides a short distance down the bank, and stops again in plain sight. The final time it sits above a pool in the river just above The Chutes and stays there. We land to scout the river, and the raven flies off into the woods.

So far these encounters have been remarkable but not truly extraordinary—a bird in distress seeking shelter in our camp, another landing on our canoe, a third that seems in some subtle way to be interacting with us. The natives of the north, though they are almost all converted to Christianity, speak routinely of elders who are known to assume animal shapes when necessary, of omens and portents delivered by wild beasts, of powers attributed to certain species—raven, wolf, fox. It is not part of my worldview, my faith, or my rational belief. Yet something mysterious and unprecedented is going on.

Eight hundred miles out we arrive at Lake Athabasca, in northern Alberta. We have 200 miles of lakeshore to get across to our wintering site. It is late August, and fall is already in the air. Wind becomes our nemesis.

This is how it goes over the next eleven days.

Day 1—Windbound after two miles.

Day 2—Windbound after six miles.

Day 3—Windbound.

Day 4—Paddle in the morning along sheer cliffs in water rough enough that Marypat pukes over the side. The afternoon calms and we get our first good mileage (18 miles).

Day 5—Windbound after five miles.

Day 6—Rise before dawn to paddle and it's calm until late afternoon (24 miles).

Day 7—Windbound in rain and sleet.

Day 8—Paddle on in rough water, rain, and sleet (20 miles).

Day 9—Windbound, snowing.

Day 10—Windbound after twelve miles.

Day 11—Rise before dawn, windbound at sunrise after six miles.

Our conversation, repeated almost daily in the tent, or next to the campfire, or standing together in foul-weather gear looking across a whitecapped expanse, goes like this.

"This is crazy. We shouldn't be here," I say.

"It has to get better," Marypat insists.

"We've been windbound on eight of eleven days, for Christ's sake! It *does not* have to get better."

"But we've still made it almost halfway across."

"Only by risking our lives. We've had a day and a half of calm water. The rest of the time has been truly scary."

"It'll get better. We just have to be patient."

"We don't have enough food to be patient. The aspens are already changing in places. The geese are heading south!"

"I just think we can do it."

"I think we should get the message. We don't have any business out on this water."

I am thoroughly spooked. It is clear to me that we are being warned again and again. Huge, lumpy swells; breaking surf; miles of cliff between good landings. Day and night of unrelieved wind. I lobby for a stop at Uranium City, the only place in the entire crossing where we might arrange a ride on a barge or airplane to get across the final half of exposed lake. Marypat is more sanguine, more relaxed, and less frightened.

After eleven days we are windbound again within fifteen miles of Uranium City. This tension that squats between us is more than the wind and waves and outright fear. It is the current spotlight of our plight together. The lake crossing is the door through which the years of frustration and waiting and thwarted hopes—the tears in the bathroom, the babies' names lost to miscarriages, the blood in the middle of the night—all come funneling.

Along the lake passage the bird encounters have intensified. In one windy camp a merlin perched in a spiky spruce fifteen feet behind the seat where I was scribbling in a journal.

The rare, swift-flying falcon stayed there much of the morning. Three days later, on a calm evening, a peregrine falcon sat in a poplar behind our tent. After dinner, as we sipped our cups of tea, the falcon flew in a line as taut as a rope into a clump of willows across from our fire. There was a flurry of small birds—sparrows, pipits—and the peregrine flapped off to its perch with one in its talons.

Along one of several stretches of forbidding, cliffy shoreline the wind lathered up huge swells. We screamed down the wave fronts in heady, terrifying rides. Waves boomed off the bedrock and snarled past the gunwales. Fear sat in the boat, as real as one of the packs.

A raven flew out from the tip of a headland. We both noticed it. Twice the bird circled out over us and then flapped into the opening of a cove. The sense of communication was as tangible as if someone were standing onshore waving a flag. Both of us understood that this dark bird was telling us to come in, and showing where to come in to. We turned into the opening without a word and coasted up onto a smooth, protected sand beach.

And again, we were windbound in weather that alternated between driving rain and wet snow. Camp was set in dense underbrush where we had finally coaxed a flame out of birch bark and twigs. The waterlogged rocks heated up in the fire and periodically exploded.

Suddenly a Cooper's hawk coasted through the willows three feet off the ground, flying slow, teetering, hunting. Its wings flared away at the last second, brushing against our blue tarp, three feet from Marypat's face. During the two days we spent in that camp, the small hawk came ghosting through several times, once landing on the fabric of our tent rain fly.

Now, in _this_ camp, the sun is warm and the sky blue, but the wind is howling through the trees. It is a beautiful little island with waves beating against it like artillery shells. We hide in a hollow and play cards. After all the hours we've spent waiting in the tent, alongshore, and around fires, we've been reduced to games of crazy eights for variety. It is a long time before the inevitable discussion comes up.

"What do you think?" I begin, after lunch.

"I don't care," Marypat says. "I don't care."

It has finally gotten to her. The relentless weather, my nagging, the fear, the strain of fighting back. She doesn't look at me and seems tired and faraway. Her hands absently pat the worn deck of cards.

"It's nothing to be ashamed of," I say. "Think of all the mountaineering expeditions that are turned back by weather or avalanche. It's like deciding not to go out driving on icy roads. It isn't worth dying for."

She just nods. Wind blows hair across her face.

In the airy silence, out of nowhere, a raven appears. Close up, the black bird seems huge. It lands in a beach of small, round rocks and hops toward us. The wings are iridescent black, the beak large and dull, the eyes shiny and piercing. It stops there, almost within arm's reach, and nails us with its gaze. Me especially.

The way the bird looks at me is absolutely personal. The raven is assessing me, challenging me, questioning me. There is no other way to put it. We look at each other for a long time. Wind ruffles the feathers on the raven's head and blows through my hair. Then it hops off and flies away.

"Have you noticed all the bizarre stuff with birds this summer?" I turn to Marypat. It is the first we've spoken of it.

"Yes!" Marypat is more prone to put stock in this kind of thing than I am. She likes to conjure up totem animals and ask questions of tarot cards. But she, too, has been reluctant to bring up these events. "The redstart on the Smoky, all the falcons and hawks, the birds in our camps."

"I even feel as if they're talking to us," I admit. "It is really weird, but at times when we need it most, these birds appear, like omens."

"Yes, exactly." Marypat is sitting up now, animated. "Like that raven the other morning, taking us into the cove!"

"This one here, just now, was the strangest yet. Did you see the way it looked at us?"

"It was looking at you," Marypat says.

It is midafternoon when we notice that the wind has died. The waves are broad swells, the sun is warm, and we pack up quickly. It is over, I think. When we reach Uranium City, we will inquire about barges that might be coming through that could get us close to our wintering site, bush planes going east that we might hop aboard.

The afternoon is lazy and warm. We paddle the alleys between islands, stop beneath an eagle's nest to hunt for feathers, and spend half an hour setting up camera shots of us in the canoe. The tension between us has dissipated as thoroughly as has the wind. We dawdle over the miles, following whims. It feels the way it used to feel, being together in the canoe. We are going to stop.

We set up camp on a long point at the outskirts of town. After dinner we walk to the top of a ridge and look down the channel we will paddle in the morning. There is a dock, a few buildings, and the loom of fuel tanks. We lean together, saying nothing, and then turn back toward camp.

"I admit, now, that I have no desire to go in there," I say as we head down toward the tent.

Marypat takes my hand. Her fingers are strong and warm. "What about this?" she suggests. "If it's stormy in the morning, we stop. If it's calm, we go on."

"Fair enough," I agree.

When I wake at dawn, Lake Athabasca is velvet stillness to the horizon.

The Armored Season

THE CABIN MARYPAT and I
kept warm and light for two winters hunkers against a stand
of poplars just south of the Northwest Territories in
Saskatchewan, nearly sixty degrees north latitude, and hundreds of miles from the nearest road that goes anywhere.
That far north it is ice, not water, that is arguably the fourth
basic element alongside fire, air, and earth. Another geographic step to the north, where forests dwindle away altogether, there are years when the ice-free season is barely
thirty days long.

Lake Athabasca is a place where freeze-up and thaw form
the bookends for winters that last nine months, where the
ways of ice dictate and inform the ways of life. Freeze-up in
the fall and breakup in the spring are the imposed pauses in
the yearly cycle. Travel depends on solid ice or open water,
so the northern vehicles—powerboats and snowmobiles,
float planes and ski planes, canoes and dog teams—are
forced to lay up at these climatic margins. By October the
boats come out of the water, hauled up on wooden skids,

their motors drained. Commonly, they won't slide back in before mid-June.

Sometimes the wait for a safe travel surface goes on for months. Months when mail doesn't come, when the hope of company is nil, when you do without. If you have forgotten to stock up with lamp oil, you make do with candles. If you run out of candles, you go to bed early. And in the fall it is black by five.

As much as these pauses are pragmatic obstacles, they are also times fraught with emotional pressure. In the fall the closing vise of winter, the fleeing life, and the gathering darkness are an accumulation of bleakness and despair symbolized by firming ice. At the same time, once the armor is settled in place, the potential to travel again and receive visitors is a relief as real as a recovery from illness.

Again in the spring the stuttering melt, the resistant and enduring layers, make for an agony of restlessness, but it is balanced against rising daylight, leafing trees, returning eagles and bears, and shed layers of clothing.

Lake Athabasca is 150 miles long and 35 miles wide. It is the remnant of an even larger body of water left behind after the final retreat of the last glacial era. It is a damned respectable remnant, and makes for a whopping ice cube.

This is how it freezes. First the fall air cools. Water at the lake's surface is chilled, grows dense and heavy, and sinks. Deeper, warmer water bobs to the surface, where it, too, grows heavy and falls, until the whole lake, top to bottom, reaches four degrees Celsius. At that temperature water achieves its maximum density, and the stirring action stops. Frosty nights are now routine, bears reconnoiter their dens, and we are busy finding standing dead jack pines and sawing them into stove-length chunks.

The cooling of the surface layer gradually continues, to a point just below freezing. Now the first ice begins to form:

free-floating, disk-shaped crystals called frazil ice. Ice crystals develop when water molecules are joined together by weak hydrogen bonds. Contrary to the way most materials act, ice expands as it freezes, becomes less dense, and floats. The crystal structure is an open lattice in which each oxygen molecule is said to have only four close neighbors. In the cabin at the end of Otherside Bay having four close winter neighbors would feel like being in downtown Calcutta, but in the molecular world it's a lot of elbow room. The frazil ice grows into frisbee-sized circles, then larger platforms, then big cakes, then fragile, jostling floes.

All this takes time. Lakes the size of Athabasca are restless, resistant beings, and wind is the common agent of rebellion. It whips up the water, bashing little cakes of ice apart. Waves pound in against the shore.

Quiet bays like ours are the first to freeze. Shore-fast ice turns into layers of sheet ice, thin and elastic as taffy, all the time stiffening, growing brittle, and getting thick. Eventually it is cold enough for long enough that the briefest lapse in November wind—a day or two, sometimes just a single forty-below night—is enough for the suit of armor to nestle insidiously over the body of lake.

Starting in late September, it is a drama to which we are riveted. In mid-October Marypat and I skate gingerly with our boots along the sheets of shore-fast ice in the still reaches of the bay. The river writhes in its channel, holding off winter a mile into the lake. The tops of rocks wear broad-brimmed hats, frozen coats of wave spray. Beyond the bay the lake is wide and black, rough and remorseless.

Frazil ice rubs together, creating miles of crystal chandelier. There are masses of it, acre on acre jingling in the margin between open water and advancing bay ice. It sounds like defiant, resigned laughter, gallows humor. Unruly waves ride through the loose mash and then plow under the elastic sheet ice like fast moles humping up dirt, until they are finally damped down a quarter mile in.

The ice cracks; new water wells up, freezes, and expands. Frozen plates shatter and shove up in ridges alongshore. Floes first batter each other and then bond together. On our daily round along the rim of the season, taking a break from hauling water, splitting wood, and chinking cracks in the cabin, we wager over the date when the ice will be solid all the way across.

Bear tracks disappear. The last bald eagle labors south through wet snowfall. The bird symphony dies away to a subdued, small-town collection of principal instruments— gray jay, boreal chickadee, raven, redpoll. Layers of split wood sheath the cabin walls right up to the eaves, two tiers thick, and it won't be enough.

Emotionally I feel myself bank the internal fires and hunker down for the dark, frigid endurance test. Our second winter confined together is underlain by a foundation as treacherous as the solidifying lake. Over the summer miles we had the travel to divert us. Here we face each other every time we turn in our burrow. Every month is a cycle of hope and depression for Marypat. The ebbing light, the deepening cold and the weeks of gray all add their thick, suffocating layers to her mood. We work together, do our chores, revel in the land, but it is superficial. Under it all lurks our long emotional winter, a season we can fall into without warning.

A Chipewyan friend from Fond du Lac, the native reserve town fifteen miles to the west, makes a visit by boat at the end of October. His is the last powerboat still in the water. We meet him at the mouth of the bay, where he yanks the aluminum hull up on a jumbled ridge of shore ice, hands us a plastic bag full of our mail, and walks the mile to the cabin for tea.

"Dangerous here," he says at one point. He juts his chin at a place we have been blithely walking across for weeks. He pulls a hatchet from his belt, walks to a precise spot, and takes two quick chops. Black water bubbles up like something eager and aggressive.

"My girl almost drowned this week," he says.

His daughter and a friend had been snowmobiling on the lake ice in front of town. It was nearly dark, so nobody saw their machine plummet through. The ice was thin enough that it kept breaking when they tried to climb out in their heavy, waterlogged clothing. Someone finally heard their cries and organized a rescue.

Every year people ride unsuspecting into bogs of slush, far from help, and get soaked trying to extricate their machines. They lose toes, feet, and sometimes their lives to the ravages of exposure. Ski planes land in lake slush and then freeze fast. There are stories of snowmobile travelers in whiteout conditions who ride full-throttle, one after another, into open leads of lake water.

One afternoon when we ski out to the high lookout point at the margin of forest, it has happened: pure white, shore to shore, leading the eye north into low rock hills and on toward the gulf of treeless tundra. A day earlier miles of gaping black lake had held off the season. Overnight it has been sealed tight as a coffin.

Along the Otherside River the turbulence of current changes the rules. Long after the lake is held down to eerie moans, tortured organ chords, and singing cracks, the river eludes winter, shifting and slippery as a mink in a rock pile.

The earliest free-floating frazil ice in river current is actually slightly more dense than water. It sinks and adheres to the bottom, where it grows into translucent submerged islands, stubborn gray masses under the hurrying cold flow. Anchor ice. As the bottom-hugging cakes grow, they slowly become more buoyant until they finally lift off, plucking up stones and grafts of streambed to take downriver.

Shelves of shore ice work slowly toward the center. Soft, gray floes jam up here and there, damming water behind them, and then break free again. Anchor ice pops up, catches under the shelf ice, and forces the river out of its banks. Current runs wild. Overnight huge overflow ponds form under the snow in side channels and marshy spots. The next day we glide into what was fluffy snow twelve hours earlier and pick up twenty pounds of freezing mush on the bottoms of our skis.

If the main channel is completely choked off, river water escapes to the surface, where it establishes an elevated course on top of the ice layers. Eventually that, too, seals up. Finally, well into December, only the deep, fast corners resist. Steam rises out of the black, muttering holes like something boiling. Crystals rime the overhanging branches with shaggy sleeves.

By Christmas the watery sounds are gone. The lake ice is three feet thick. The river is subterranean, a thing heard through crevasses. Our neighbors begin to move about in their winter patterns.

At our south-facing windows, through which we can watch the entire low arc of the winter sun over the ragged spruce trees, we watch for wild entrances onto the icy stage: A lynx at twilight, gray as the day, body sloped down from hips to shoulders and built to sprint after its only prey, the snowshoe hare. Red foxes and tar-black silver foxes, leaving erratic lines of tiny tracks like sewing machines gone mad.

One morning we are getting water from the hole we have chopped in the ice when a wolf appears out of the forest and starts across the bay. Another follows, then another, until there are four of them strung out across the opening—long legged, tawny white in the oblique sunlight, their breath rising in smoky puffs.

They stop in a group and face us. Thirty yards apart, we are looking into each other's eyes, hearing each other breathe. Ice crystals in the atmosphere make a prismatic halo around the weak sun. I lean on the iron spud bar we use to pound open our water hole. One of the wolves sits on its haunches.

There is no sense of threat in the air, no menace wafting our way from these lean and wild beasts. I have the strong impression that they have taken our measure, sized up whatever emanations we exude, and come to the conclusion that we can be trusted, from a distance.

It is a long, quiet time before the sitting wolf tips its head and begins to howl. The sound is a low, hard-to-place moan, like distant wind. Then it grows into that primal lament, that fierce joy, a sound that fills the dome of sky. None of the other animals joins in, and when the howling wolf stands again, the small pack turns and trots away.

We leave our own marks on the country—ski trails up the river ice that parallel the belly slides of otters, cross the beaten paths of wolves and foxes, and wind through the terrain of urine spots, melted circles left by warm, napping bodies, and bark stripped from willows. We weave through patches of plump, grouse-sized night burrows of willow ptarmigans, cratered fields in the insulating snow.

By midwinter the water hole is four feet deep. The ice chunks and water we shovel out each day crackle like breaking glass as they land. Steps chopped in the walls of the well allow us to reach the buckets down. The same hole provides the rinse cycle for hand-washed laundry, pants and T-shirts that freeze solid into contorted mannequins as they emerge.

Inside the walls of our den we balance the need for companionship against the hunger for solitude. We are held in a sixteen- by twenty-foot space, cluttered with our supplies, where we are almost never more than ten feet from each other, month after month. But whole mornings pass while Marypat practices her drawing at one table and I scribble at another. It is exactly the way in which, paddling the canoe together, we can drift apart mentally at the same time that we push our craft in a straight line across the wordless miles.

Admittedly, there are less content interludes. Times when cabin fever is an emotional malaise, when something as inconsequential as the way Marypat eats or my habit of pacing the floor as I think provokes outbursts of frightening anger. We face off then, glowering at each other as if everything is at stake. A kind of madness inhabits the air until one of us stomps out for a walk, leaving the other entombed by desolate loneliness.

The snowmobile trail for the fifty-mile run between Fond du Lac and Stony Rapids goes past the mouth of Otherside Bay, about a mile out on the broad lake. In the open spaces the ice is full of wind-drifted waves, or *sastrugi*, frozen humps of packed snow marching in step with prevailing winds. People routinely drive forty and fifty miles per hour, speeds that make your tailbone ache and your face freeze in white patches. Once in a while someone detours in to our cabin, braving the wind-deposited drifts of snow and the lurking pockets of slush: Chipewyan natives on their way between settlements, a local Royal Canadian Mounted Police officer and his wife out on a weekend jaunt, a game warden weary of the trail. They bring mail, local gossip, and hunks of caribou meat, and we babble at them, prisoners starved for company.

Some years, if the ice is strong and the demand for merchandise is high, a temporary road is punched north long enough for a convoy of semitrailers to steam across the lake. The string of trucks follows a snowplow, and the snowplow follows snowmobiling point men armed with ice augers. The scouts range ahead, taking core samples and calling out the best path by radio.

The trucks never shut down. They follow each other at prescribed distances. Too close and their combined weight is dangerous; too spread out and they lose contact, risk being blocked by drifts that can close the road as fast as it opens. At a certain spacing they can set up harmonic vibrations similar to the ones sometimes generated by winds hitting a high bridge. Waves start to undulate through ice that is three and four feet thick, rolling and heaving in slow cadence beneath the truck wheels until it is like driving through the middle of an earthquake.

The trucks rumble out of the gray-white distance and into Fond du Lac or Stony Rapids like wagon trains appearing out of a prairie blizzard, delivering tons of disposable diapers, cases of soda pop, chain saws, propane bottles, and frozen pizzas.

For the most part, winter is silent as the inside of a cave. When trees, their fibers tortured by cold, pop in the night or when a raven croaks in the gauzy sky, it is like someone shouting in a library. The silence is so deep it is the inner sounds one hears—the heart pumping, a vague sea roar in the ears, warm breath hitting cold air.

It is mid-February when Marypat tells me she thinks she's pregnant.

"You are not!" I explode. "Jesus, MP, how many times do we have to go through this?" I am really angry. So much of the time I am a bystander, waiting for her signals. So much of the time there is literally nothing I can do. I want to get on with it, get our life back, have Marypat back. "You're just late again. How can you even think you're really pregnant?"

We don't speak of it again, but Marypat is centered somewhere else, somewhere interior, another place I can't go. A week goes by. The time for her next period comes and goes. She is queasy during the day. I shut away the temptation to hope.

Sometime in late March the river begins its summer song. It is faint at first, a stronger chord beneath the thick plating. Then the shallowest rapids open. Early thaws soften the snow in the woods and add melt to the watershed. Patches of ground appear, collecting warmth like solar panels.

The winter landmarks by which we have known our territory begin to evaporate: otter slides and dens, the trail made by a moose grazing in willows, the violent place where an owl pinned down a ptarmigan—wing beats, spots of blood, scattered feathers. And our own signs—webs of snowshoe prints, mile after mile of ski tracks.

At first these landmarks are set in three-dimensional relief as the softer snow melts around them. Ski trails turn into elevated rails six inches tall; then they soften and lose their definition.

After months spent bundled in silence, spring is a dazzling clamor. As soon as the river erodes a short channel into the bay ice, there are bald eagles circling and crying in search of fish, otters sunning at the water's edge, snow buntings pecking at the rotting snow, killdeers searching the open ground for nest sites.

Marypat's belly is slightly rounded. She has vague pains, quirky hungers. When she is three months along, we spread the news in the letters we send south.

At night I lie spoon-like against her back and lay my hand on the smooth swell of skin, this bud. We couldn't have done it back home, I think. It took this winter, this year away, this leap into the abyss of wilderness, both ours and the land's, to accomplish a fetal heart. It is a gift of place and of season. I know this truth.

Bears come back. At dawn one morning a black yearling

is peering in the front window of our cabin. Later, across the bay, I watch an adult stand up and waddle into the alder thickets, grab an armload of shrubbery in a hairy embrace, and pin it to the ground, where it licks off catkins with a methodical, mobile pink tongue.

The urgency of season is too much for us. We exhume the red canoe, drag it over snowdrifts to the edge of open water, and take it out for daily laps. Tundra swans float, sedate as white ships, in the open bay. When they lift off the water their wings sound heavy as thick, flapping canvas. There are eared grebes, blue-winged teals, and snow geese in the water, western sandpipers and water pipits alongshore, and a short-eared owl standing far out on the gray lake ice.

There are nights when I can't sleep for the excitement. I pull out the maps, against my better judgment, and start scouting north and east along the summer's trail. I have looked at enough maps, compared them with enough country, that the sheets of paper are powerful evocations of the landscape I will soon come to know, full of esker ridges, driftwood fires, thundering falls, arctic terns, and the sweet slide of canoe hull. I pay for my weakness with a restlessness that rises in me like the currents that are gathering everywhere in the spring bush. Only my overflow has nowhere to run.

Then I am assailed by doubt. How can we go on? How can we risk the baby, after all we've come through? But is it really a risk? I see us deep in the tundra, Marypat bleeding, a primal sadness settling over us. We decide that we will make the forty-mile paddle to Stony Rapids a trial run before we confront our decision.

The lake is the last thing to go. The mouths of rivers open up. Then gaps along shorelines where rocks absorb sunlight. Twenty-hour days turn the implacable surface to gray, pitted dinginess, but winds coming across it are still reminders of January.

Even into May the daredevils in town snowmobile, and it's June before the surface finally breaks into huge floes. Then it is the wind, the same airy blasts that hold off ice in the fall, that finishes it off in the summer. The wind herds the gigantic rafts here and there, grinding them against the shore. An ice chunk ten feet square and a foot thick weighs almost 6,000 pounds. There are floes of unguessable weight on Lake Athabasca, ten times the size of our cabin and four feet thick, battering rams at the whim of gales.

By mid-June it is really over. We load the canoe as if to head on north. In the Barren Lands there are still snowdrifts the size of houses; it will be another month before the big lakes are unshackled. We paddle off on faith that the way will clear in front of us. Faith, in fact, is coming to be our operative theme.

In less than four months the first crystals of frazil ice will float again in the chill, black waters of Lake Athabasca. Shelves of ice will harden in the broken rocks along Otherside Bay. Life will stream away again, refugees in front of the advancing season, until only the bears curled in clefts of rock, the fish growing lean in the depths of lake and river, the wolves howling into the brittle sky remain.

Perhaps, too, the flame of a single, warm candle will shine out through a cabin window, a place both prison and sanctuary, miles from anywhere.

Eskers

WE ARE EIGHT DAYS down the Kazan River, and Marypat, six months pregnant, is napping again after lunch. She is curled on her side, head on her life vest, on the barren crown of this island. Sorted pebbles the size of marbles surround her. The ground nests of sandpipers, plovers, and terns occupy shallow scrapes in the gravel, full of eggs so pebblelike that we have to walk storklike, studying the ground, before we set our feet. She is wearing a pair of loose green overalls, tundra maternity garb, with the cuffs tucked into her socks to thwart black flies.

Our decision to push on in spite of, or maybe in honor of, the pregnancy has changed everything. The year of wilderness therapy, the summer full of birds, and the plunge into winter have come, now, to this. We are together, completing the cycle. Only now there are three of us along for the ride; one of us is mute and unformed but no less present. In the tent at night we feel the elbows and knees of our baby punching at the walls of its dark, fluid room. Marypat, the risk taker, was more confident about striking across the tundra than I was, but the life gathering inside her has made her more tentative than usual. She is uncharacteristically timid and nervous before minor rapids. The tendency to slip into a combative state of mind and take chances when the winds pin us down or the weather turns bad is so clearly inappropriate that she never falls prey to it. We take our time, take naps, stop to snack, wait things out.

It is a state of mind that we strive for on most trips but which the baby has made unnegotiable. The baby, and the clean rhythm that comes, finally, from being out on the land for 400 days. So it feels, this summer, more like living here than traveling through. Because of that we are more aware than ever of the things that do live here, and of the ghosts of the Inuit.

The People of the Caribou gave birth in their igloos and skin tents in this spacious, wind-harried, scraped land. They lived, for all purposes, a Stone Age existence here fifty years ago. Women carried their children in the hoods of their skin coats, held hungry mouths against their breasts, sewed small clothes against the coming winter. Time and again we move among their tent rings, their stone hunting blinds, their rock-pile graves. We are not doing anything new or exceptional.

How to explain this new dimension of awareness? We are open to things we never were before—interactions with inanimate objects, access to ritual, communions unique to this time and place. We are centered here more than ever before. When winds keep us in camp, we make offerings to the waves with bits of dried caribou meat given to us by a native woman at the start of our journey. Being open, we receive. It's as simple as that.

Another strange thing. Time and again the eskers draw us to them. They are the sand rivers of the Barren Lands, gravel ridges that coil over the unpeopledness where jack pine and poplar and spruce give way to the tundra, as if the world were a mountain rising up north and as if, as on a high mountain, trees couldn't stand the height. Eskers sprawl across the skeletal landscape like the casts of unearthly burrowing creatures. They trend here and there with no apparent regard for topography, meandering across lakes and rivers, wandering over hillsides, transecting drainage patterns.

Some of them are hundreds of miles long, sinuous ribs of sand and gravel, vestiges of the glacial era. On maps they are drawn in like narrow, black, furry caterpillars. The best guess, and there is some serious mystery about eskers, is that they are the deposits of glacial meltwater, made up of the sand and gravel carried along and dropped in the icy tunnels carved out by powerful meltwater rivers. They pay no heed to modern topography because the water that flowed off the big ice sheets responded to that ephemeral terrain, not to what lay underneath. They are the representation, in horizon-spanning Braille, of glacial drainages.

In the Canadian expanse of permafrost, tussock-filled ground, insect hordes, swamp and muskeg, and stagnant pools that is, overall, about the size of Alaska, eskers are a benison. They offer high points where a couple hundred feet is a commanding elevation; walking surfaces free of muck and ankle-twisting hummocks; denning sites for wolves and grizzlies and arctic foxes in country otherwise unfit for digging and lying in; windy ridges where the clouds of mosquitoes and black flies are beaten down. A relief to the eye. An invitation to get out of the canoe and use our legs. Places to nap.

As on the day when we paddle up to a long esker that cuts across a nameless lake on a nameless little river in the Keewatin District of the Northwest Territories. The esker there is visible for many miles, a shining white ridge looping off across country and almost damming the lake, except for a narrow pass where the water pushes through with a slight current. The gap is tight enough that we aren't entirely confident of the passage shown on the map until we come within a quarter mile and see the blue pinch taken out of the ridge of sand.

A fog of insects rises out of the moss as we step out of the canoe. They follow us to the top of the esker ridge, where the slight breeze strips them away. We pause there, refreshed by the wind, turning to look out over the boulder-strewn distance. The boulders are another inheritance from the glaciers, an assortment of rough-edged rocks—granite, quartzite, gneiss—dropped aimlessly like scattered furniture on the tundra floor. Erratics.

Inevitably there is a trail along the gravel spine, as there has been on every Barren Land esker I've ever ascended. Wolf scat mark the prominences—some white with age, others fresh, full of hair and bone. Caribou horn, fox track, grizzly print, all present. A northern shrike, its hooked beak sharp as a claw, watches from the stubby dead spar of an ancient tree two inches in diameter.

We walk and walk. It is irresistible: views of green moss, blue water, white sand, gray rock, pale sky. I am still getting used to Marypat's profile, her rolling gait, the way she moves gingerly on her hips. Far behind us is the red speck of our beached canoe, patient as a mule. These views, always, are pregnant with possibility—the brown shift of grizzlies pushing through willow bottoms, wolf pups at the mouth of a den, the antlers of caribou limned against the sky.

There are wolf dens in these eskers that have been occupied for more than a quarter of a millennium. Scientists have dated the bones left at their doorways. Fifty years before the Declaration of Independence the ancestors of the wolves that howl along this esker may have lapped the wet fur of newborn pups in sand holes just below our feet. It is a reassuring continuity, a pleasant reality check.

Finally, at a high spot miles down the ridge, we sit together on the warm, lumpy surface of a couch-sized boulder. Marypat slides her hands under the heft of her belly. We don't speak. Life buzzes around us, but not human life. There is no fence line over the brow of the ridge, no road in three hundred miles, no town, no cattle, no condos. It is a place awash in space and the brief, fierce flowering of summer, free of the human hum.

A place and time in which I can fathom the possibility that rocks have spirits. The rock we sit on, for that matter: warm in the summer sun, carried here in the icy talons of a glacier about the time, perhaps, when humans were discovering agriculture along the Euphrates River. It has been rubbed against by generations of grizzlies with itchy shoulders, peed on by wolves, and slowly cracked by the worrying dark frosts each winter. A thing alive, with history, incorporated into a community. It is a thing that might, at that moment, sense our weight and feel our cool shadows fall across it.

A thunderhead works toward us, shiplike, from the horizon. We stand again. Before starting back, I lay my hand on the rock, exchanging warmth. Then Marypat and I move on down to our red plastic boat, to the shafts of wooden paddles working our callused palms, to the sentient water furrowing beneath the hull. Back to maps fuzzy with errant tracks of sand rivers.

Barren Lands

HUMANITY IS A WHISPER here. Here caribou breast the landscape in antler-bobbing streams. Here musk ox pound craters in the snow with their chins to reach winter grass. Wolverines and arctic foxes scent through the mosses after small prey—lemmings, tern eggs, hares. Sandhill cranes court one another on low bedrock ridges with stick-figure decorum. Here a wolf plunges its face into the hot entrails of a caribou calf. Here winds comb the stiff-grassed tundra with restless, rough, currying fingers.

Humanity is elsewhere, gone away, sloughed off to the coast like the draining rivers taking their load of sand. Starved out, decimated by smallpox, swindled by the fur trade, and seduced by religion, rifles, whiskey, sewing needles, sedentary comforts. That old story. That old story no one wants to hear and I don't want to tell. A story that makes my bones heavy.

Only this faint stirring in the air remains: the whisper of ancients only a generation past. They were still here, clothed in skins, dancing in igloos, beating on drums, welcoming the first birds of spring, walking the ridges, and spearing caribou at river crossings, when I was a young boy learning to ride a tricycle in a Boston suburb and John Kennedy had a decade yet to live.

I have met them. Grandmothers who clean hotel rooms in places like Rankin Inlet and Baker Lake but who, as young girls, pounded strips of caribou into dry meat and competed with the foxes for birds' eggs. Old men who return to the land once or twice a year by powerboat or snowmobile to shoot caribou with .30/30 rifles but who, as young boys, paddled skin kayaks and carved snow blocks to build igloos.

And on the land, the swell of northern land, a crescendo of teeming emptiness, I have had the company of their whispers.

At a windbound camp on Kamilukuak Lake, when I stoop down to pick up a piece of weathered driftwood and find that it has been worked, fashioned to some purpose—weapon, tool, piece of boat frame. My hands run over the surfaces painstakingly crafted by other hands, hands separated from mine by an unimaginable gulf of circumstance, yet focused on the same smoothed stick.

Or paddling across Angikuni Lake toward the outlet of the Kazan River. There on a low, broad ridge stand a series of *inukshuk,* the rock cairns built across the treeless terrain to signify trails, caribou crossings, campsites, and graves. They pluck at the corners of my vision. Again and again I turn to them, expecting to see one raise an arm in greeting, to see another break into a run.

Again, in the Thirty-Mile country, when we stop for lunch and there are half a dozen tent rings, rock circles that once weighed down the edges of caribou-skin shelters. I lie in the center of one, on ground that cushioned the sleep of an Inuit family, a man and a woman, children: people, I think, satiated with the land. I think that because scattered everywhere on the ground are old caribou bones settling into the sphagnum.

Or on a wave-washed rock beach along the shore of an unnamed lake, where a low pile of rocks, full of gaps and crevices, hunkers just above the high-water line. Inside, the gleam of bones. A human femur, rib slats, the top of a skull. Gray lichen feathers around the cranial sutures.

We were here, it all says. We lived here. In our way we flourished in this immense scarcity. We made love on this ground, bore children in this tent. We stood, just here, looking across the same blue-seamed space, knowing that space. We wrestled dead willows to kindle our fires. We stooped over grizzly tracks in the sand. We lit moss wicks steeped in caribou tallow to flicker against the winter night. We listened to the singing ice in the fall and thought of the meat cached away in permafrost crannies. And always we awaited the caribou, watching and listening and scenting for them every day, and dreaming of them by night.

Near the end of our yearlong journey, Marypat and I stop on an island to stretch our legs. It is that time in a long trip when the finish looms near and we resist, we dawdle, we let our food run low, staying an extra day here and then deciding the wind is too strong to fight the next day as well. Marypat is seven months awkward. She moves as if she's aged thirty years since her midwinter declaration. The paddle rubs against her belly on every stroke. She asks for a hand to help her hoist herself out of the tent each morning. Her face is round as a drum. The impending birth is the only thing pushing us to get back.

It has been long enough that we feel suspended, half feral, deep into a space we must leave. A space that has brought us close again. This is what it is like to be converted to a strange, compelling faith, to believe without doubt. The idea of our return is a thing we abhor, and the whispers are damn near audible.

A flat bench partway up a ridge draws us to it, where we turn to take in the view. At our feet, sunken in the ground, are foreign pieces of wood. Foreign because there is no wood anywhere in many miles. We haven't seen a tree more than head high in a month. The driftwood we make our fires from is the thickness of our fingers. The only trees are wind-twisted, ground-hugging, spruces barely waist high. This is real lumber, six-foot lengths, one-by-four boards, and once we spot it, a litter of it snaps into focus all around.

At first the wood appears milled, finished with precision machinery. I pick up a lichen-encrusted board and see, close up, that it is actually rough-hewn, almost perfectly turned but done by hand. On the inside surface is gouged a row of evenly spaced, angled divots. The cross pieces cut to match those divots have fallen almost exactly in place. They still fit neatly. In fact, laid out there on the ground, fallen apart yet in a recognizable shape, as if a carpenter had set out the pieces of a project each in its approximate position, is the frame of a kayak.

These bits of wood may have been collected and passed on for generations. A well-turned cockpit combing would have been an inheritance worth marrying for. There is not a screw or a nail anywhere. Whittled pegs still protrude through holes drilled out with a primitive bit. The curved boat ribs, the support pillars, the long sides, the keel, all are there among the moss campion and short, bristly grasses.

It is as if a carpenter had fashioned all the parts of a project, set them in place, and then never gotten back to it. Or, and this comes to me as I stand there in the summer warmth with black flies pinging against my forehead—it comes looming up out of the whispering past with the certainty of a true and real story—it is as if an Inuit man, a hunter of caribou, had paddled his skin-covered craft up against the same sloping shore where our canoe rests.

I T IS A FALL DAY in this story. The lake is black and choppy, the sky lowering, the wind like shafts of ice. Flecks of spray have frozen like candle wax where water splashed up on the deck, on the sleeves of his skin parka, on the leading edges of the wooden paddle blades. A young boy ducks out of a skin tent and runs to join the man onshore. Together they lift the boat and carry it up to the flat, protected elevation. They pause, with the kayak at their feet, and look across the dark water. A thin snow scuds across their view.

Winter comes. The long twilight, then true darkness. The lakes freeze like plates of iron. It is a starving season. The fall caribou hunt was a marginal success. Hunters waited at the time-honored river crossings, hunkered behind rock blinds, but the deer never came. Only a few meat caches are full, and the wolverines pillage one of those. The oil lamps run dry. People sit in a dark stupor, in semihibernation, for days at a time. Sickness visits the camp; people wither and shrink. A young woman dies in childbirth. Elders walk out of the igloos in the night and don't come back. Late in the season, still months from spring, the people abandon camp and straggle toward the wan hope of a distant fur-trading outpost.

Spring arrives. The ice rafts up under the lash of wind. The sun is buoyant, high in the sky. Birds fill the open water; gravid caribou push their way toward calving grounds. The kayak rests patiently on the island. Its decay is a slow, gnawing dissolution made up of freeze and thaw, chapping winds, chewing rodents, the insistent settlement of fungus and moss and lichen.

The stretched skin goes first, that thin organic layer; then the sinew thread in its small, tight, meticulous stitches. Rodents den up in the hull and raise young. A two-year-old herring gull perches for much of a summer at the tip of the bow. Bird shit, fish bones, and eggshells litter the ground. The sun dries the skin to parchment and desiccates the exposed wood. Every winter the snow drifts over the boat, forming a white burial mound. Water fingers into the cracks and then freezes, prying the boat open.

When the young boy who helped stow the kayak after its final outing is a father with children, a man who lives in a prefabricated plywood house in Chesterfield Inlet and whose bad dreams writhe with emaciated ghosts, the first board drops loose. The next winter a peg falls out. The hull surrenders its form to the erosion of time and gravity and chance. The wood, precious and rare, settles its small weight into the tundra, and moss rises up around it.

WE PLACE THE PIECES of boat frame back into the perfect molds on the ground. My hands tingle with this communion, paddler to paddler. I have been out long enough that the lift of waves under boat hull is a sensation branded into my nerve synapses. I have felt the same cords of river current bending past rocks, dropping over ledges, eddying alongshore as this paddler did. I have hunched down against the same implacable winds roaring across a plain of water. I have paddled into the midst of grunting strings of caribou swimming at a blue narrows, felt the close thrill of their straining bodies. I stand, now, in this paddler's footprints and look out across the blue expanse, the gray, distant hills, the patches of snow that linger, even in August.

When we paddle away, I notice the feathery contrail of a remote jet in the cloudless sky.

Part III

Confluences

Gravid Miles

EXACTLY ONE YEAR after our communion with the tundra, I am settling our firstborn into the bow of the canoe, and he is not pleased. Eli Kazan Kesselheim is eight months old, harnessed and tethered to Marypat, lathered with sunscreen, and wearing river shoes the size of teacups. The canoe nods in the current below Yankee Jim Canyon on the Yellowstone River in Montana. Eli displays his robust lung capacity as we shove off for a month on the water, an interlude long enough for us to descend the entire watercourse to its confluence with the Missouri.

Fifty strokes downstream he is asleep, lying on a pad between Marypat's feet, with the river tickling away at the bottom of the canoe hull an inch under his back. I'd like to think that he is recognizing the river motion, that he is comforted by the roll of current and lift of waves. He has already felt a thousand watery miles slip past from the remove of the dark, liquid world inside his mother. On the tundra, in Marypat's womb, he was most active at night while we slept in the tent. During the day, in the canoe, he was still; sedated by the restless, watery rhythms. At eight months he has experienced more water than many people do in a lifetime.

The same family members and friends who thought we were reckless and insane to continue our expedition in spite of the pregnancy think we are reckless and insane to set off on this first family boat journey—four weeks on the water with an infant. It's all in the perspective. To us it seems no more risky than strapping him into a car seat and joining a stream of heavy metal projectiles hurtling along at seventy miles per hour. Less risky, in fact.

It's not that we are never crippled by doubt. In fact, we could easily have been dissuaded from completing our long northern journey because of Marypat's pregnancy. Late that spring on Lake Athabasca, we had trekked the fifteen miles into the medical clinic on the native reserve in Fond du Lac, Saskatchewan for a prenatal appointment with the doctor who flew in once a week. More important, we sought his advice about the wisdom of traveling on.

In the examining room, Marypat lay flat on her back with her rounded belly exposed. The doctor placed a black amplifier on the curve of skin. Marypat's eyes closed. There was static, intestinal gurgling, and then something coming on clear and unmistakable. That infant heart—fast, steady, gushing, working away. Marypat grinned in recognition. Her hands moved up involuntarily to her belly.

"Sounds good," the doctor said. "Steady and strong."

We had many questions, fundamental doubts to address. Marypat propped herself on her elbows and explained our dilemma to this stranger. He listened carefully to the outline of our itinerary, Marypat's description of the physical challenges, the daily routine, the portages. I could tell that he knew nothing at all of the remote tundra, or of the regimen of wilderness life in a place where we wouldn't see a single human all summer.

"The pregnancy is just fine," he said when Marypat finished. "You're past the first-trimester worry of miscarriage and you'll be out before you have to worry about early delivery. A woman should be able to continue her normal activities through most of her pregnancy. This might be exceptional for many women, but it sounds pretty normal for you. I can't say there isn't a risk, but you're obviously in good shape, and you've thought about this carefully. There are risks anywhere."

As we left the clinic, Marypat turned to me, her eyes lit up and cheerful. I knew that she was still hearing that gushing, confident drumbeat inside her.

"We can do it," she said. "I really think we can do it!"

If it had been a different doctor that spring day, a doctor who questioned our plans, who chastised us for our unconventional approach to prenatal activity, or who stressed the risks over the normality of pregnancy, we would never have gone on. Our plans ran directly counter to conventional medical wisdom, which tends to view pregnancy as a disease to be treated in hospitals and a woman's pregnant months as her period of confinement. If we had chosen to cut our expedition short, if that had been the precedent, it is also doubtful that we would now be embarking on a long paddling trip with an infant who can't yet walk.

What the world doesn't know as we catch the pulse of the Yellowstone and Eli naps in the bow, and what we are hardly discussing yet ourselves, is that Marypat is pregnant again. There is another throbbing bud inside her, barely begun, yet responding in some primordial way to the river we ride down, picking up signals, reading the water, sensing the weather. This time around we see the trip as a kind of fetal baptism, a blessing.

Eli was born in our bedroom, with the help of a midwife, two months after our return from the Barren Lands of northern Canada. Marypat labored for the better part of a day. It was snowing outside. When his head finally came out, I slipped my hand underneath it. With the next contraction I caught his wet, slippery body. His blue eyes were open, he hardly cried. Before we even knew his sex, we wrapped him in a towel and he went to nursing, his clear eyes fixed on Marypat's.

After his birth the doctor who had worked with Marypat through her years of infertility told us it was highly unlikely we'd get pregnant again. "People will tell you stories of women who finally had a baby and then couldn't stop getting pregnant," she said, "but it's a myth. Marypat's in her late thirties. She's nursing. If you want another child it will almost certainly take as much time and effort as it did with Eli, if you can do it at all."

Seven months later, steadily nursing and without any intention of getting pregnant, she missed her period.

Marypat knows her body, has a sense of her limits, and can feel the tune of her physical self as acutely as a musician knows the sound of her instrument. On the Seal River that first summer of our relationship, she took to paddling with the same grace and skill and eager confidence that she has brought to rugby, swimming, sculling, and softball.

During the northern summer, with Eli growing inside her, I eventually learned to drop my cautious solicitations. Marypat took her turn in the stern of the canoe as usual. She trundled off across portages bent under the sixty-pound packs I lifted for her. I came, over the weeks, to trust her intuition. She is a physically competitive person, but she also knows when to back off. By the end of that summer we were plodding across the portages and stopping to rest every quarter mile, keeping each other company. The pregnancy pace, we called it.

When she needed to nap, we stopped. If she had some

quirky hunger pang, we took care of it. If it took twice as long as normal to get across a portage, so be it. From the outside perspective—the perspective our families had—our endeavor no doubt seemed risky, even foolhardy. From inside the canoe it seemed to us absolutely sane and right, just as the first miles on the Yellowstone with an infant and a burgeoning human seed feel sane and right.

Being in a canoe together, reeling up pieces of water, is what we do. It is the vehicle we choose, as often as possible, to reckon with and to escape from the paved world. I once read about a doctor who worked in the jungle back country of South America. He had two young children, and the children did what he did. They slogged through swamps, cowered under deluges, peeled leeches off their feet, and slept out on viny trails: dangerous, risky stuff. And they thrived doing it.

We do boats and water. Other people do cities and subways.

We have traveled a thousand miles of northern tundra and five hundred miles looping across Montana, all the way with stowaways tucked in for the ride. Stowaways with hearts beating as fast as a bird's, who get their own doses of adrenaline in the rapids, who slosh around in their slow, liquid dance to the tune of rivers diving for the sea.

What we don't know on the Yellowstone is that it isn't over yet. Three years later we will have two boys, Eli and Sawyer, in the canoe, toddlers as comfortable in boats and tents as they are in cars and houses, and Marypat will be seven months pregnant with our daughter. The fertility advice will be wrong again. Ruby will thrust her way into life despite contraception, and despite the fact that I have scheduled my vasectomy appointment for the week after Marypat discovers she's pregnant.

Ruby's fetal river benediction will be held over a two week

stretch on the Rio Grande along the Mexican border, in Big
Bend country. Big Bend will also serve as an apt description
for the way Marypat looks when she ties her shoes.

On each of these trips Marypat reaffirms that the river is
the best place for her to be. In the wilds she is centered and
undistracted. Much of the time I have the distinct impression that she is listening hard to some interior song that only
she can hear. It makes me feel like a deaf person watching a
conversation.

It is exactly the way I felt during the years of infertility
and, later, the way I feel when Marypat nurses each of the
children. I am an outsider, the donator of sperm. Marypat
rides the hormonal swells, shares her blood and food, feels
the urgent pull on her breasts, hangs on during the agonizing push from impossibly tight canal into life.

By the time we're through, Marypat will log nearly 2,000
pregnant miles. In a strange, disorienting way it will come to
seem that these rivers—the Kazan, the Yellowstone, the Rio
Grande—are actually how we got our children. The water
journeys are intertwined with the birth journeys: parallel,
symbolic, feeding one another, each cleaving toward life.

That day in northern Saskatchewan when we wrestled
with the decision to plunge ahead during our first pregnancy, it felt as if we were weighing whether or not to put our
child in harm's way in order to indulge our selfish hunger for
adventure. But once we were underway, and over the next
years, it felt as if we were bathing each of our kids with our
greatest gift.

Border Flow

O<small>N THE SURFACE</small>, at least here, there is nothing to distinguish the Mexican side of the Rio Grande from the American. On both banks the Chihuahuan Desert lifts away—creosote flats, bristling acacia trees, prickly pears the size of outhouses, century plants, and layers of gray- and peach-colored limestone eroded into pits and sharp points. Cactus rock, the locals call it.

It is our second day on the river. The mouth of Santa Elena Canyon, a slot in the sky, rises up ahead. The campsite on the southern shore, on a low bench shaded by acacia shrubs near a small tributary, looks better than anything on the northern side. We stop and set up camp.

We drove 2,000 miles to get here, braving four days in a Subaru station wagon crammed with all our gear, a canoe on top, and two small, fidgety boys inside. Our car has studded snow tires. When we left Montana it was twenty below and there were two feet of snow on the ground. Marypat is seven months along, top-heavy enough that when she shifts in the canoe it can be alarming.

At first sight, bumping down the steep dirt incline at the put-in, the river was an anemic bleat of grandeur, neither Grande nor Bravo, as the Mexicans call it; a narrow, muddy meander we could drive across. We have been told that the region has been suffering from an eight-year drought, and it is a desert to begin with.

I have hiked to the treeless, wildflower-lush ridge in the San Juan Mountains of Colorado where the first trickles coalesce into the seams and runnels of clear water that become this river. I have rafted through the turbulence of the Taos Box, where the Rio Grande is a churning exhilaration in the depths of a sheer canyon. I have lost my clothes capsizing in a rapid along the edge of Bandelier National Monument. But none of that water makes it this far.

The Rio Grande drains a watershed the size of France that is notable for its unrelieved aridity. Much of the drainage receives less than ten inches of precipitation per year. Moreover, as it descends through Colorado, New Mexico, Texas, and Mexico, it is siphoned off, greedily suckled at by irrigators, industries, towns, and cities. Just downstream from El Paso and Ciudad Juárez, it runs dry in the sand. The river is gone. Hundreds of miles from the sea, it turns to dust. The water that flows along the border of Big Bend National Park is almost entirely supplied by the Rio Conchos, rising in the mountains of Chihuahua, deep on the Mexican side. Mexican water, such as it is, drought weary and nearly nursed to extinction.

We left the Subaru in the shade of a thatch awning in Lajitas. By the time I had hiked the half mile back to our canoe, I was sweating in the February heat.

Eli and Sawyer love our camp. To them, this place is not another country; it is a riverbank with a good perch of limestone from which to throw rocks into the river. Sawyer is not yet two, only weeks out of diapers, and he is already straining to keep up with his three-year-old brother. The boys each have a low-slung seat nestled amid packs in the canoe. Their little day packs are crammed with trucks and plastic dinosaurs, and each has an inflatable whale to trail alongside the canoe on a string. When we stop during the day we fill their plastic buckets full of rocks, which they plunk over the side as we paddle. For them, canoe travel is nothing remarkable. The boat is simply another vehicle, more fun than a car.

Before dinner we explore a small slickrock tributary behind camp. The waterworn rock is smooth as porcelain, rubbed to a dull shine. Marypat hoists herself over the lip of a small pour-off, huffing for air. She is round as a beach-ball and giggles ruefully.

It is twilight when I hear the sound of horse hooves on rock, then voices. In the amphitheater of silence, sound carries for miles. It is a few minutes before I finally spot two riders on the lumpy skyline. When the breeze wafts our way, the clop of hoof against rock sounds as if it were next door. I hear the banter, in Spanish, of two men. Then the noise fades away again. They are making their way along a rim behind and above us.

Our red canoe is turned over onshore. The blue-and-white tent, and our colorful packs stand out against the sand. I know, even before they turn toward us, that they will come into our camp. It is a disquieting knowledge, a stirring in the bowels, for reasons I can't articulate. Two horsemen, strangers from another land, are coming to us in the dusk. Before long they begin picking their way down through the ledges. It is an arduous, thorny route, and there is no conceivable reason for them to come that way other than to visit us. They are taking their time. I see now that they are a large man on a horse and a skinny companion astride a donkey. The animals shift their way closer through the desert.

In 1988 a couple and their guide on a raft trip in Big Bend were ambushed by gunfire from the Mexican side. The husband died instantly from a spinal wound. Both the woman and the guide were hit, but they managed to reach land and crawl for cover. The woman passed out behind a rock, but the guide was able to escape and bring help in time to save her. Eventually three young Mexican men were apprehended. One of them is still serving a life sentence.

News accounts tended to pass over several provocative events, perpetrated by Americans, that may have led to the attack. In one case a Mexican horseman had been shot from his mount. Another horse had been shot and killed. Then a woman carrying a water bucket had been shot at from the U.S. side.

The border here is more than a cartographer's line across the landscape, some arbitrary, politically mandated scribble along an arc of latitude. It is a parting of geography by water, a margin essentially rooted in topography. Drainage, in the desert, is everything. The lines in the sand. Where water runs, where it pools, when it is abundant and scarce, and who gets it—these are matters of life and death, health and sickness, fertility and barrenness.

This border also separates people who speak different languages, who celebrate different holidays, eat different foods, sing different lullabies, and organize their days around contrasting concepts of work and leisure. People whose thoughts chug down divergent tracks. One land is comparatively rich, the other poor. That is the nub of it. Poverty and wealth, real and imagined, underscores all the rest and drives the fundamental, inescapable tension between cultures.

Our canoe is probably worth more money than either of these twilight horsemen makes in a year. Taken together, the value of our gear, our camping outfit, might be enough for a family of subsistence farmers to retire on. The idea of traveling several thousand miles with your entire family, floating a river for the fun of it, and then returning home, staying in motels along the way, is as conceivable to the Mexicans living along this remote and parched strip of desert as building a spaceship.

By now our attention is focused entirely on the riders. They have stopped talking. Branches slap against chaps and saddles. The horse grunts with the descent. Marypat and I stand together, next to the tent. Marypat rubs the inside of my arm in a nervous gesture. The boys have been playing in the sand, but they stand up and look, too.

"Horsie," Sawyer says, pointing. Eli nods solemnly.

The lead rider is a very large man, unshaven. His belly rivals Marypat's. His chaps are of thick leather, stained and worn and scored with thorn scratches. He ducks and weaves through the lethal acacia shrubs. Close up, the men seem to be moving more quickly, looming over us. I see them assessing. Their eyes rove through the camp, taking in the two small boys. I see the large man's eyes rest on Marypat. Then the dark horse is in our midst, crashing through the thicket. The rider leans forward, face against mane, to miss the inchlong thorns. The horse prances sideways past our tent, shying at the color. We stand still. The boys' mouths hang open.

"Hello," he says, lifting his wide hat briefly. His smile is awkward, a little sheepish, and his horse never stops. At the steep little draw next to camp he spurs the animal down the sheer gravel bank and up the far side through a seemingly impenetrable screen of prickly brush. He laughs while doing it, more a yell than a laugh.

The donkey rider is an old man who says nothing. Maybe he's not old; maybe he's fifty and will look the same ancient, leathery way for another thirty years. He smiles at Marypat. His teeth, those that are left, are brown stumps. When he reaches the draw, he decides better and dismounts, shooing the donkey ahead. The old man hobbles across, and calls his donkey to a stop, and then swings up again, stiffly, his legs dangling.

The two men ride up a steep, narrow trail to a rim and then disappear. We hear their talking and the hooves on stone until it is nearly dark. I wonder how far they will have to ride through the thorny night and what story they will tell when they get home.

SANTA ELENA CANYON is a place no one goes except by boat, riding the liquid international trail. Its sides are absolutely sheer. When you lie on the sand at night and look up, the stars are a bright, narrow strip, an avenue of sky. The river is in shadow for twenty hours every day. The one major rapid, called the Rock Slide, was created by rocks that rolled from the cliff walls directly into the water. Most rapids are formed by boulders washing in from a tributary, or from a constriction in the river channel, or from a particularly steep section of gradient. This one is made from rocks the size of rooms that fell from the sky.

Moments after we stop at the head of this limestone chaos, a raft coasts up, carrying two young women and their guide. I have no idea how they made it down this far. The river has been punctuated with bumpy little rapids, shoals with two inches of clearance, and constrictions we were hard pressed to get a canoe through. The guide must have every deep channel memorized.

He goes down a straight chute that leads into the jumble of boulders and then pivots into a pool that he later tells us is called the Texas Gate. Normally the Gate leads into a set of tight maneuvers, but at this water level it is only a pool dammed by a ridge of gravel we will all have to lift over.

Marypat and I follow, backpaddling, the canoe's stern

angled in against the shore. The water is so shallow that it's hard to get a good purchase with our paddles. The current pulls us hard toward the first angular rock. The bow actually thunks into limestone briefly, and I am momentarily disabled by a mental image of tiny life vests being sucked under the stone, before we slip into the pool.

The rest is anticlimactic. The river moves in a slow, stunned way among the obstacles, and our canoe glides through the slots at the canyon floor. But the raft is another matter. The guide and I stand in water up to our waists and wrestle the fat rubber boat almost up on its side before it will scrape through one of the narrows.

"I don't know how we can run it much longer," he says when we part.

Where the canyon opens up again a day's journey later, the temperature jumps twenty degrees and the light is brilliant white. We stop at a shaded campground to replenish our drinking water and decide to spend the night. There are flocks of white-winged doves, a roadrunner, and the clatter of cottonwood leaves in the breeze. We are the only campers with a tent. Everyone else is a snowbird in a motor home whose overwhelming obsession seems to be getting the rig parked level. We cook our meal over the camp stove to the hum of generators and the smell of charcoal lighter fluid.

Across the river, out of sight, sits the tiny community of Santa Elena. For a dollar, a man in an aluminum rowboat will take you across. His oars are shafts of metal conduit with squares of plywood bolted on the ends. The village sits a half mile back in a cottonwood grove. The houses, made of timeless, weathered adobe, are spread along a dirt street. There is the inevitable plaza, with a gazebo and concrete benches, where men gather in the shade to discuss the universal topics—weather, sin, schemes. Electricity has just arrived within the past decade, supplanting traditional street-corner socializing with families clustered in living-rooms watching *Dallas*.

Big Bend is as out of the way as a national park gets. Roads dead-end at the river. The nearest community of any size is Alpine, Texas, an hour and a half's drive north. And Alpine is a helluva reach from anywhere you could call cosmopolitan with a straight face.

From Santa Elena it is a six-hour round trip on dirt roads that anyone with any sense would call four-wheel-drive tracks to reach Ojinaga, upstream and across the river from Presidio, Texas. Several times a year families from Santa Elena go to Ojinaga to shop. Education beyond the third grade requires that children find a family to live with in the city. Consequently, most residents have third-grade schooling. People often live their entire lives within a hundred-mile radius.

Before the border was anything more than a river, the crossing near Santa Elena fell along an Apache trading route. The trail crossed a low nick in the Sierra Blanca to the south, descended to the freshwater spring, crossed the Rio Grande, and pushed on north.

In the morning a couple from Indiana insist on driving us to the river in their motor home. Eli and Sawyer scramble aboard and make short work of exploring the appliances and cupboards on the two-hundred-yard trip to the canoe.

"You *all* fit in there?" the woman asks. "In that one little boat?"

Three major canyons—Santa Elena, Mariscal, and Boquillas—punctuate the border float. Between each we paddle for days, all alone, through the open desert. We become expert at deciphering the deepest channels, but we still have to wade over shoals here and there. Big Bend turtles sun on logs and muddy rocks; catfish the size of footballs lie half out of the water in the shallows.

Canoeing is not the meditative rhythm it was in the pre-child era. Several times a day, when the boys get restless to the point of distraction, we pull over to stretch. Eli and Sawyer set immediately to manicuring the sand into roads and castles. They are addicted to throwing rocks at the water, the universal sport of toddlers.

We have stern discussions about the correlation between scorpions and the undersides of rocks, but we never uncover one. Everything here has thorns, a sting, or poison to inject. In the fall tarantulas migrate in such numbers that the roads get slick with their furry remains.

The broad country bequeaths views of the Chisos Mountains, an island of volcanic rock rising out of the sea of desert. Lower down, the landforms are abrupt, resistant juttings from the volcanic era—Elephant Tusk, Mule Ears, Cerro Castallan—dark intrusions punched up from somewhere unimaginably violent and heated.

At our hot camps we strip off our clothes, dip in the viscous water, and come out encased in a thin sheath of mud. Within days we take on a dusty, aboriginal look, a desert varnish. Park brochures advise against contact with the river. The coliform counts aren't what they are in El Paso, but immersion is frowned upon. Across the way residents dip in their buckets to water their vegetable plots and wash their dishes. At one place a pickup truck loaded with fifty-five-gallon drums is backed into the river, and two women in long dresses are ladling water aboard with coffee cans. Who knows what was once in the metal drums, to say nothing of the river.

The economy along the southern edge of the Rio Grande is made up of subsistence farming and ranching, small back-country camps devoted to cooking down candelilla cactus to make high-quality wax, and smuggling. Illegal drugs and migrants get all the press, and there is a significant flow of both passing back and forth, but the majority of contraband is less glamorous fare—refrigerators, clothes, pickup trucks, television sets, various armaments.

The crossing at San Vicente is rumored to be the hub of the smuggling trade, and when we stroke past there is a line-up of pickup trucks aimed toward Texas. It is a male place. Teenage boys rove restlessly along the gravel bar. Men lean against open truck windows, talking. The place has the aura of an enclave with its own politics. There is a lazy tension in the air, a watchfulness, palpable even at midriver.

At the entrance to each of the canyons it feels as if the boat is diving into a cool tunnel. Once we are inside, I hold back, savoring the time within walls. There are canyon wrens singing their fluted, liquid song. The river livens up, bumps into walls, and swings hard around corners. We stop often to explore tributaries, these keyholes into the subterrain. I am drawn to the southern ones. They seem more likely to have mountain lions, and there is no danger of our running into an Audubon group strapped up with Nikons and exclaiming at Mexican jays.

Sometimes the excursions become dead ends within a quarter mile, truncated by sheer walls that are like burnished iron. We lay our hands on the smooth stone and stroke it as if it were skin molded over hips and shoulders. Other tributaries we ascend for hours, bellying over lips, skirting falls along ledges, and hauling the boys up smooth ramps that they immediately want to turn around and slip back down, like otters. Despite the prolonged drought, there are occasional protected pools, called *tinajas,* where water is trapped during flash floods and where maidenhair fern drips down the cool rock. Sometimes, miles from anywhere, we stumble across old candelilla camps with rusted fifty-five-gallon drums, bits of wood, and fire scars.

The farther up these sere arteries we go, the stronger the

pull of the umbilicus gets. The urge to turn back, to return to the flow, is as real as a thirst.

At Rio Grande Village we stop only long enough to refill the water jugs and buy the boys ice cream bars. By now the river has us. We load the water into the canoe in an alley of head-high river grass and shove off again without saying a word to anyone.

That night the winds come. Afternoon breezes escalate to a buffeting gale that rips the tent stakes out of the ground. We have to weight the windward corners down with five-gallon water jugs, and all get inside, to keep the shelter from rolling off downriver.

It goes on for two days. For the first time it feels like winter—not cold, exactly, but raw and exposed. The paddling takes on a distinctly uphill quality. The boys wear coats and winter hats pulled over their ears. They jam their hands into their pockets and hunch into their clothes, stoic as little old men. Sand peppers our food, sifts inside our sleeping bags, and collects in the corners of our eyes. Everything is granular. On the second night we find a camp in a quiet wind eddy at the base of a cliff. Three steps in any direction and we bump into the hurricane, but we live, for the night, in a bubble of calm.

Back in 1535, one generation after Christopher Columbus made his landfall, a Spaniard named Cabeza de Vaca was wandering around in the Rio Grande valley. He was the treasurer of an ill-fated expedition that set sail for the New World in 1527. After years spent floundering around in the Caribbean and along the East Coast of the United States what remained of the expedition was shipwrecked off the coast of Texas. Cabeza de Vaca endured the life of a slave to local Indians for several years before escaping with three companions.

The small party of men wandered throughout much of

the desert Southwest, gathering fame as healers among native peoples, before finding their way south to a Spanish outpost in Culiacán, Mexico, in 1536.

Along the way de Vaca recorded a place at a great river (the Rio Grande) where there were "many houses seated on the banks of a beautiful river." The Indians brought him a man who suffered from an old arrow wound. In an audacious surgical feat, de Vaca managed to cut out a long arrowhead and suture the wound closed.

"The next day," he wrote, "I cut the stitches and the Indian was well." The cure made de Vaca so famous that he was followed around by throngs of natives sometimes numbering in the thousands. He wrote that "it was very tiresome to have to breathe on and make the sign of the cross over every morsel they ate or drank."

In our exploration, near the downstream border of the park, on the southern side, there is a young boy checking a fishing line marked with oversized bobbers made from empty milk jugs. He stands up to look at us, hands curled at his sides. Then he bends over, lifts a string of catfish from the ground, and holds it up, the dull fish glinting in the sun. He is dark and lean, curious and alien. Our boys stare back. Eli lifts his hand to wave. Behind and above the boy, inside a crude wooden fence made of sticks, are a couple of goats and a donkey. The house is a one-room square, a building made of the desert.

Around the corner there are rangy cattle with wicked horns and bloodshot eyes, wild as javelinas. Animals wander back and forth across the river, poaching forage on the American side. To the delight of the boys, we coast through a small herd of horses standing belly deep in the water. The park does little to enforce its boundaries. How could it?

This quadrant of northern Mexico is a gaping, arid emptiness the size of Louisiana. There is one road coming from the south to the town of Boquillas. Outside of that, the terrain is all dirt ruts and cattle trails. On maps even the watercourses look dry, drawn in with a series of intermittent, unreliable dots. Ramparts like the Sierra del Carmen run in north–south scars.

Ranches on the American side are vast spreads the size of small countries. It takes a hundred acres to support one cow, and the land gets overgrazed at that. The big operations have their own airstrips, their own machine shops, and maintain a system of roads.

Our take-out is the bridge at La Linda. The man we contacted to do our vehicle shuttle wanted to know exactly when we would get off the river. He doesn't want to leave our car unattended for more than a few hours and certainly not overnight. We slip through the cool band of shade under the bridge and pull in to a rocky bar, an ending as anticlimactic as they all are.

Within three minutes I spot two young men walking toward us from downstream. I keep unpacking the canoe. They come up, smiling, and say hello. Using gestures, they indicate that they want to help us. They want a job. We smile back and shake our heads. One of them points to Marypat and gestures that she shouldn't be lifting anything. He reaches for a pack. We laugh and say no again. They insist. We shake our heads.

For a minute we look at each other, with the river muttering by in the heat, and then they shift back a step, turn, and drift back downstream over the muddy rocks.

Spring Dance on the Gallatin

MARYPAT IS WEARING a wool hat, a vest, and a windbreaker. She cinches up her life jacket and picks up her wooden paddle. We look at each other.

"Ready?" she asks.

"I guess." I move toward the knot that holds the canoe in check.

For some reason it occurs to me that we haven't danced together in a long time, years maybe. Dancing is how we met, in large measure how we fell in love, but I wonder if we could regain that magic, find the rhythm again. I wonder if I really want to know.

Several times a summer we prevail on family or friends to take the kids for a day, and then escape to a segment of water we would never try with children aboard. We escape to paddle the way we used to paddle, to have one or two days away from the diaper-changing, dispute-settling, bill-paying, spill-cleaning, laundry-folding, storytelling, swing-pushing life harnessed up to three small children.

Escape is a relative term. It isn't really the way it used to be. There is that small extra caution in every move on the water that is made up, at the root, of our knowing that those lives are, in every way, attendant to ours. The cord never cut.

I hear impatience in the sluicing, cold river water. The Gallatin, where it lopes over the northern boundary of Yellowstone National Park, is high and loud with the melt that has been imprisoned since fall in high-country snow and ice. The bank-full stream sounds reckless as desperadoes on the run. Damn the world anyway, it says. I'm free for now; come along or get the hell out of the way.

The red canoe sits in a narrow sliver of an eddy, tied to a slender willow. The boat nods and bumps against the tether, anxious as a spring-shy colt. I don't share the same impatience as the swollen flow, nor the light eagerness of the boat. I am still heavy with accumulated winter sloth, extra pounds, creaky joints, and the dark densities of the cold season, like dangerous boggy spots in the thawing interior landscape.

Snow clings in gray patches to the slopes just above the river and still lies deep in wooded thickets. The breeze carries a winter scent, and I think of the pair of gaunt elk listlessly feeding in the bottomland near Taylor Creek, their ribs standing out like barrel staves. They hardly lifted their heads as we drove past.

We settle into the canoe and take the first strokes away from the bank. There is that strange, niggling unease common to all our childless interludes, as if we've forgotten something big. The river's careless strength is a surprise. We bump on a rock, the current grabs at the upstream edge of the hull, and we have to brace hard to regain balance. We're not dancing yet, not by a long shot. The river is an impersonal strength, an impartial power, and it is bigger than we are.

Above Taylor Creek and all the way up into its headwaters, the Gallatin is a smooth slick of river, winding fast and steady against grass and willow banks over a gravel bottom. Below Taylor Creek it is all boulder garden and rapid, wave and emphatic eddy. Most of the year, and all year when the runoff is low, this rocky upper stretch isn't worth the trouble. Running it at low water is like playing pinball and being the ball. But when the runoff is strong, for a brief window of time, it is a spring run to wait for through the dark, frozen heart of winter.

Beneath Snowflake Falls, where warm water weeps down the hummocky green slope, we take a side channel barely twice the width of the canoe. It is a bobsled run, with hard turns against grassy banks, and we start to get our timing. Marypat leans out on a draw stroke at the head of a corner, I pry the stern around, and we schuss into the next straightaway.

"Nice. Really nice," I say to myself, not as a compliment, but because the motion, the lean of boat and the certain grab of current and the soundless turn, are so utterly sweet.

Being in a canoe together is the other way we fell in love. It's the same way, really, because the river flowing and the beat of waves and the blended percussion of strokes that takes us here and there on the water is dancing, too. Just as sure as rock and roll. When it's right, when it's good, the canoe is an appendage as alive and responsive as our arms and legs.

How do people share a house, eat food together, sleep belly to back, and yet drift apart? Weeks go past between times when I really see Marypat, when it's more than passing on the stairway carrying laundry or a dry kiss on the way out the door. Longer still between flickers of that old heady energy we can generate together, that thing that is greater than two.

As we go under the highway bridge, backpaddling away from the center piling, the river changes. We pivot the canoe clumsily into an eddy you could park a semi in below the first big rock we've seen. It isn't a pretty move, as eddy turns go, but we've arrived; we're starting to play off each other. I can't see Marypat's face, but I know she's grinning when she plants her paddle back in the murky flow and the boat turns smoothly downriver again, picking up speed.

Taylor Creek is a thick, muddy brown cascade coming in from the west, roaring off the slopes of the Taylor Peaks and washing in its load of rock and sediment. The Gallatin turns from a big stream into a small river right there. The two flows run side by side, distinct shades of brown refusing to mix. The river is suddenly full of rocks and standing waves, and the noise is a throaty drumroll that we have to shout above to be heard.

But we aren't talking much. I watch Marypat's strokes, sense her body language, see the routes she's picking, and follow her lead. In the stern I take the longer view and choose our general course, aiming toward the outside of the next bend, or to the left of a gravel bar, or along the base of ledgy cliffs. The canoe sideslips above a boulder and then dives down a narrow "V" of water; we slow down to coast through a set of waves and then eddy out against shore to breathe and bail the sloshing collection of splashes. The motion is a constant, fluid, dynamic flirtation with power.

The Gallatin is the color of bad truck-stop coffee. Clouds move quickly overhead. In succession it hails, rains, drizzles, and is bright with sun. A winter-killed mule deer lies on the bank, bedraggled as a wet rug, settling into the earth. Mergansers stand on the tops of boulders and wing downstream ahead of us, just above the wave tops. Spotted sandpipers run in the stones at the river's edge. They bob and peep and pick at food in Charlie Chaplin double time.

The miles that roll under us are at once familiar and full of surprises. For a decade we have paddled this stretch of water every year when the runoff has been strong. I remember the choices where the river divides at a small island—one channel is a straight shot through waves; the other, a jumble of rocks. I see a spindly fir that is still maintaining the same impossible levitation it has for years, sticking straight out over the river, hanging on against gravity and the slow, inevitable picking away of the bank. But there are also new deadfall in the river, spring logjams, reconfigured rapids, and blocked side channels.

We have logged thousands of miles together now, hundreds of days making boats move along beneath sky. It is like something saved away, a wealth, an accumulation to dip into: the way Marypat leans back as we ram into a wave; her square, strong shoulders twisting for a cross-bow draw; her irrepressible giggle that bubbles out at the head of a long chute; the way, when we've nailed something at the edge of our skill, that she whips around to look at me as if it's the first, best time and she wants to be sure I am there with her. We are richer at every bend.

The canoe dodges and weaves through a mile-long rock garden and then slides beneath the low bridge at the 320 Ranch. My legs are wet from the knees down and my fingers are rigid with cold, but we have a momentum now. It is a good rhythm, this piece of river, and we are lost in it—the canoe is wearing us and we are wearing it. It feels as if we're dancing every song in a long set, our moves mirroring each other's. The energy rises up, better than warmth, and breaks out in the inebriated grins we wear. The band is hot, the floor shakes, and neither one of us wants it to stop. So we don't stop, not until we eddy against the bank below the bridge at Red Cliff. By then it is only adrenaline that keeps us warm.

Adrenaline, and the realization that somewhere in the wordless tumult and sweet motion we have lost the dead spaces between us, the gray decay of winter.

A Fly-Fishing Tradition

My BROTHER-IN-LAW and my fishing guide for the day, Paul, has just handed me his $450 graphite fly rod with a pretty convincing show of nonchalance. I strive for the appropriate affectation of practiced ease. Sawyer is with me for the day, standing nearby in his little life vest, waiting the way all children learn to wait for whatever is coming next. In the ongoing negotiations that surround parental labor, it is understood that Marypat will get time on the water at some unspecified future date in return for granting me this fishing outing on the Madison River.

While Paul busies himself readying the drift boat and fussing with gear, I wander through a deja vu moment. I am a kid again, standing near my father along the Stillwater River, upstream of Nye, Montana. Dad's gaze is concentrated on the dense selection of fake barbed insects lying in the worn leaves of his leather-bound fly book. He plucks one, mysteriously, from the jumble, deliberately ties it to his line, and settles himself, already lost in the study of water, intent on eddy and rock and pool.

It is exactly the same feeling here today on the Madison, as if a spotlight has narrowed the world to this self-absorbed circle of boat, equipment, and people. The everything-in-its-place fussiness; the specialized gear—vests, boxes, reels—which bears the same aura as Dad's fly book, cane creel, and worn waders. Even the air has the same taste and smell, potent with that expectant, hunting edge.

But it is not, for me, a moment for wallowing in pleasant nostalgia. Despite having a father with a passion for casting flies, despite having lived near premier trout water for healthy chunks of my life, and despite writing a column for a magazine that carries a fishing ad or a fishing photograph on every third page, I have managed to avoid the fly-fishing mania. In fact, I've developed something akin to a distaste for the sport.

It isn't that I don't have a few fishing stories. Mine have to do with skewering bright orange salmon eggs on a hook and plunking them unceremoniously in the backwater behind a boulder or hunting grasshoppers in the hot brown August grass, feeling the live, prickly spring of their legs against my clenched hand, and jailing them in a jar or tin until I am so caught up in the hopper stalk that I forget about fishing.

When it comes to fly-fishing itself, my stories are mostly not about fishing at all. They are not about that electric moment of contact with a trout, nor about selecting the perfect bug for the day and presenting it in such a way so as to be irresistible, nor about careful approaches, impossible casts in willow thickets, or unexpected spring creeks thick with huge, line-snapping fish.

No, my fly-fishing anecdotes mostly involve some degree of physical pain, overwhelming boredom, or humiliation. In them I am shinnying up a sharp-barked spruce that I've snagged about twenty-five feet up on my back cast or dinging myself on the top of my head on the forward cast. Or, worse, I am catching a companion by the clothes, under the chin, or by the ear; spending twenty minutes sweating over an impossible knot before accepting the obvious and snipping the line; or hanging out, there on the bank, while Dad does the patient angler routine till sundown.

So, when Paul has the boat all set and says, "Let's have a quick lesson before we get on the river," I am not overcome with a flush of eagerness.

He handles the gear with that deft sureness so daunting to the casting impaired. He strips out line, flicks it here and there, and sends it over the water in singing loops and dainty landings. He instructs on the importance of mending line, pausing on the back cast, following the drift. He seems to be paying no attention at all to his movements but to be all the time watching the river.

He hands the rod back to me. "You're a natural!" he effuses after I try a few practice casts. I'm not having any of that. I've heard it before.

As we clamber over the high-sided gunwales of the drift boat and settle ourselves—Paul at the oars; me standing, braced, in the bow; and Sawyer in the front swivel seat—I am resigned. At least the September day is warm and beautiful, the water clear, and the cottonwoods burnished yellow. We will enjoy the day together, despite the fishing.

In Montana, fly-fishing might as well be the state religion. The sanctified dogma is catch and release. To disdain the piscatory sport, under the Big Sky, is tantamount to avowing atheism. Never mind the evidence that catch and release is, often as not, more like catch and maim or that some 15 percent of caught and released fish die from the trauma. Never mind, either, that the reverent handling lavished on cutthroat trout and arctic graylings is decidedly lacking when it comes to bottom-feeding whitefish and catfish, which are frequently left on the banks to expire.

The elite of the angling world gussy up in fancy regalia— fishing vestments, if you will. They cross continents in pursuit of waters blessed with certain ordained finned lifeforms. They lavish entire vacations and wholesale hunks of their savings accounts on the quest.

They stalk, they scheme, they lie in wait; they employ skills built up through hours of video viewing, front-lawn casting workshops, guides' tips, and the inevitable accumulation of tree-climbing, snarl-snipping humility that is the lot of budding fly-fishers. They are daily aquiver with that hunting thrill. Then, at the end of the day—ruddy from exposure, whipped by shrubbery, senses tingling with the memories of glinting swirls and jarring strikes and whiffs of trouty bank— they go home and grill up a steak.

When I go fishing, I am hunting down food for dinner. The avocation as art form or therapy doesn't compel me in the slightest.

Our float begins with Paul saying that he can't understand how people can simply go down a river without doing anything. "There's always something to do when you're fishing," he says. "You're always busy."

Just about then, barely out of the shadow of the put-in bridge, I tie the line in a snarl the size of a Ping-Pong ball.

"Always something to do, all right," I mutter as Paul drops anchor.

For a while it looks as though we'll never get out of sight of the car. The anchor goes up and down a handful of times, the fingernail clippers hanging from Paul's vest are put to use cutting line, Sawyer gets restless, and I start imagining all too clearly what his first fishing memories will be made of.

Eventually I make a few consecutive casts without

mishap. We lose sight of the bridge and Paul takes up his patient instruction, a sort of angling catechism.

"Lay it in just above the boulder," he says. "There. Now, in the slick below. Mend your line. Mend. Mend! Cast. Again. Great. Let it drift. Mend your line. Good drift."

Not often, but occasionally, his voice quickens with excitement. "There it is! Now!" And I set the hook just a beat late and fling the fly thirty feet behind me.

No matter. It is a lovely day, one of those fall gems aching with the poignant warmth of summer, with the river settling toward its low ebb, with the boat nodding to the timeless rhythm. For someone with my angling legacy it is enough to be here, making a reasonable show of it, staying out of trouble. Catching a trout hovers near the bottom of my agenda.

I even start believing Paul when he gushes over my natural talent. Those moments are short-lived, though, because as soon as I settle into a more self-confident posture, I am abruptly brought up by a clumsy, flailing attempt at a long cast. Once, when we are close to shore, I wrap the line around an overhanging cottonwood branch in a secure knot and am caught in yet another ignoble moment, an addition to my extensive archive of humiliating memories.

After a while I find myself losing interest. I am repeatedly diverted by osprey nests, a mule deer in the cottonwoods, and a growing urgency to sit down and enjoy the drift. Paul is possessed with that predatory focus, that unflagging gaze, that barely relaxed set of tension, always ready to strike.

He is one of a class of Montanans who manage to make their living by means of various predatory vocations. His freezer is always brimming with the meat of game shot during a late hunt or by virtue of an out-of-season permit or during a special antelope season. These opportunities to hunt seem to go on pretty well year-round, if you're vigilant enough. When he isn't filling the larder, he is guiding for the droves of humanity who come here to gun down big game or to flail the blue-ribbon trout streams. Occasionally, and only under financial duress, he succumbs to carpentry work.

We switch from a Prince Nymph to a Dave's Hopper and then to a Parachute Adams. Paul becomes gently impatient when I miss a couple of opportunities.

"It's not exactly hot today," he says, "but we've had our chances."

We drift on. I miss another. "The boat rule is that you buy the guide a six-pack for every fifteen misses," Paul announces.

"You want a turn?" I offer generously.

"Hell, no; you've gotta catch some fish!"

Sawyer is amusing himself by clambering back and forth over the swivel seat. For a two-year-old he is remarkably patient in boats, but it has been a while since our lunch stop, and it's clearly time for a diversion. The pressure mounts.

But it's almost worse once I manage to coax a few modest trout out of the river and into the net. Sawyer suddenly understands what this is all about and rises to the occasion with enthusiasm.

Now it's "C'mon, Dad, catch a fish!" He is gripping the gunwale eagerly, watching the fly with the fierceness of a ferret at the mouth of a prairie dog burrow.

"Here, fishy, fishy, fishy," he calls. Then, exasperated with my incompetence, "C'mon, fish, jump in the net!"

I admit that it's fun to catch a few, but in hundreds of days spent on rivers I've been able to occupy myself perfectly well without lobbing barbed armaments into the water. When I offer Paul another chance and he accepts, it is a relief to sit at the oars. This is something I know: how to move a boat across current, how to turn into an eddy, what the river is communicating up the oars, up my arms, into the gray matter, so that it is all of a flowing piece.

It is a relief, too, not to pay strict attention to the blindered angler's world, confined to the snaking filament of line laid out, again and again and again, with that ersatz bug on the end of it, to the exclusion of all else.

At the end of the day I am not a convert. In fact, I am not in the least swayed. I am, simply, a flyaphobe with a few leavening memories of success, who has been indulged on a rich fall day, whose son has at least a hope of escaping his father's fishing fate, and who cheerfully buys the guide a couple of six-packs.

Seeking the Wild

OUR HOUSE is two blocks off Main Street in Bozeman, Montana. The fire station is less than three blocks away, The Bowl is directly through the backyard, the Salvation Army is around the corner, and the federal building is a five-minute walk away. We are along the funeral procession route to the cemetery.

One winter morning I found deer tracks on the frosty front sidewalk: a trail of cloven hoof prints, heart shaped and unhurried. It was early. Mine were the only other tracks in the crystalline snow. The deer trail had the look of tracks made by a neighbor quite comfortably at ease. The kind of tread we leave on the way to work, or heading around the corner for a newspaper.

Each print was sharply, firmly, and daintily defined. The deer went straight down the center of the sidewalk at a composed walk, minding property boundaries, better mannered than most dogs. There had been no startled leaps, no detours; not once had it broken into a trot. Past the new bed-and-breakfast that has all the neighbors talking. Block after block along the same route I walk almost daily to check the post office box.

Sometime later I began thinking about finding wilderness, wildness, in unexpected places and about the wildlife that has penetrated into the bewildering thickets of our civilization. Elk mingling with Herefords in fields south of Bozeman. Mountain lions within an easy lope of the capitol in Helena. Coyotes in the hillsides around Los Angeles. In the wilderness, when I see some elusive animal, a bear, say, or a pine marten, I wonder how many other eyes are on me that I am not acute enough to notice. Now I wonder it on Olive Street.

It must be a daunting frontier, full of inexplicable noises and confusing odors, lethal missiles of steel, fences, blinding headlights, pavement, roving packs of dogs. Think of it: descending from the cool, forested high country, finding a way through the zone of cultivated private land, moving on past the ring of suburban tracts. Following stream beds, traveling at night, reading the sensory topography. Finally, entering the innermost center of urban growth. Then imagine working out a way to flourish there—discovering food and shelter, negotiating a network of trails, avoiding the many strange dangers, getting water, finding kin, raising young. Two blocks off Main Street!

I keep my eyes open now. From the ridge near the cemetery overlooking town I have watched groups of deer leap along a shrubby stream course. A red fox in a town field recently locked eyes with me as I drove past. A sharp-shinned hawk once landed on the roof rack of our Subaru, and it regularly makes predatory passes over our backyard bird feeder. There are elk pellets on the suburban ridge I walk every spring to see the new crop of wildflowers.

They are among us, making whatever sense is required out of the unruly thing we call town.

More and more I try to follow their example. Backcountry, in surprising vigor, is in the midst of urban and suburban landscapes, where we last think to go. And there is a deliciously smug satisfaction in finding it under the noses of work a day crowds, virtually in their backyards. It is like Clark Kent and the phone booth.

My current favorite is a little stretch of the East Gallatin River. It is close enough that I can get down it in a two-hour time slot, as if working out at a health club. I put my canoe in the water at the Humane Society Animal Shelter and take out at the bridge next to the wastewater treatment plant; about as urban as landmarks get. In between it is fast, hard-bending creek where nobody goes, full of surprises.

Sourdough Creek, which flows through the heart of town, an aberrant blue squiggle defiant of our right-angle organization, comes in just upstream. Rocky Creek, Bear Creek, Kelly Creek, Meadow Creek, and a dozen more ephemeral dribbles have already added their water, but the East Gallatin is still small enough to be dammed by a single toppled cottonwood. Although it has barely gained respectable momentum, barely gotten its name on the map, it has already run a gauntlet of indignities. By the time it courses past the animal shelter, it has been through the back of the local stockyard, run past a Superfund site, and been siphoned off into an irrigation ditch.

There is a rutted dirt pull-off where I unstrap the canoe, carry it down to some thick-barked, river-guzzling cottonwood roots, and set it in the quickening flow. Abruptly downstream a dead tree blocks off two-thirds of the river. Suburban this run may be, but if I'm sucked into the branches of deadfall it won't matter that I'm within city limits.

One quick bend downstream and it no longer feels as if I'm in town, either, no matter what the zoning maps say. The banks are thickly overgrown, full of yellow-rumped warblers and goldfinches. A great blue heron raises its prehistoric form off a gravel bar, wings like gray leather, neck like a snake.

I have to watch myself. The East Gallatin hurries to leave town, determined to join the rest of the watershed and, in short order, to add its contribution to that river of destiny, the Missouri. The bends are sharp and overhung with brush. Snags poke out of the shallows, and the current is combative.

There is concrete riprap along the banks, along with rebar, whiskey bottles, old refrigerators, tractor tires, and the ubiquitous shreds of plastic. On an open bend I glimpse the modern trash heap, the city dump, hulking on a hillside overlooking the valley and filling up fast. Then I see a stretch of manicured grass, the new golf course going in. But just then three sandhill cranes fly low overhead, burbling their unmistakable call, in search of a grainfield or resting spot or simply making companionable talk on their way to the Arctic.

Bridger Creek banks hard left and spills in, almost as big as the Gallatin itself. I pick my way through a ghostly maze of whitened, debarked, river-lodged trees, a dangerous and lovely corner. This is exactly what I need, being here. The knots that tie themselves tight over the days of town life start to loosen up. I can feel my face relaxing. Ideas bubble up, as if they've been shut up tight and need only an open crack to slip free. On the mud banks there are the hand prints of raccoons, beaver-chewed trees, and an old sofa buried to the armrests in silt.

Suddenly, around a hairpin bend, a logjam blocks the entire river. I am a dozen feet away when I see it. The river is pushing eagerly. I backpaddle hard, angle for shore, and clutch at the willows to hold myself. A huge cottonwood is firmly wedged from bank to bank, collecting a dam of branches, small trees, and garbage. I haul the boat across the muddy neck of land and put in again, my guard up. There are more trees downstream, narrow passages through branches and stumps, tight corners with current undercutting the banks.

The river winds and coils. I catch glimpses of the Bridger Range and then the Spanish Peaks, Hyalite Peak, and a weathered barn. For a stretch there are a great many old cars embedded in the channel. Hudsons, Willyses, Dodges, one-ton trucks—the vehicles our parents drove and then tipped into the river when they quit. There are trout nosing gearshift knobs, silt sifting into seat springs, turtles warming on exposed rooftops.

Once or twice I eddy out behind these artificial boulders. The river doesn't know granite from steel, and the water swirls back on itself just the same. The bow of the canoe bumps as restlessly against a Model T bumper as it does against Precambrian quartzite.

Then it is over. A final tight corner with small standing waves, and I am back. I clamber up the concrete-strewn bank upstream of the bridge and am welcomed by the set faces of my neighbors inside the cars speeding past. Most people don't notice me. I am still in town, but it feels as if I've popped back up through a manhole cover from a secret, unvisited wilderness.

I strap the canoe to the roof rack and quietly blend with the traffic. I don't even leave tracks.

Flood Watch

OUR FRIENDS Ursula and Dee Dee bought the old, bunged-up farmhouse on five acres for more money than they like to admit. Paradise Valley, south of Livingston, Montana, and smack on the bank of the Yellowstone River, is hot property these days. In the hunt for land, you compete with buyers with names like Forbes and the Church Universal Triumphant.

Ursula, a former neighbor and a godparent who helped with the home births of all three of our children, was finally making good on her threat to give up two decades in the landscaping business. Dee Dee was leaving an acting career in Seattle. The house was a hundred years old and looked it. Previous owners had let pets run inside, overfilled the outhouse, and let the small barn go to ruin. The wallpaper was stained and peeling. Sections of rotting floor sagged underfoot. The plan was to transform the building into a bed-and-breakfast. The River Inn, they'd call it.

Fifteen steps from the back door the Yellowstone River rolls past. An island of willows splits the channel there, and a wide braid of river shunts against the bank, a channel big enough that it takes a good arm to hit the island with a rock. An eddy the size of a porch circles just upstream, a place where guests might cast for trout of an evening. When we went over to see the place for the first time, in late summer, the boys were down playing on the sand beach next to the swirl of river within thirty seconds.

"It's never flooded," Ursula said. "They say it's on the hundred-year floodplain, but it's never been wet."

"Either that's good news or you're due any time," I said.

They spent the better part of a year, and pretty well doubled their investment, transforming the place. They raised the roof and tucked a couple of bedrooms with attached baths underneath. They stripped the walls to the studs, pulled up the floors, replumbed, rewired, dug a new septic system, and refurbished the well. They built rock gardens and flagstone patios, added porches upstairs and down, and put in horseshoe pits. They dragged over a sheepherder's wagon and fixed it up for guests with a hankering for the rustic and a more affordable night's rest.

They called one suite the Yellow Rock Room, another the Absaroka Room. From upstairs you can see up the valley along the jagged, snow-touched peaks of the Absaroka Range, all the way south into Yellowstone Park. From anywhere in the house, if you open a window or door, you hear the river nosing past over the cobbles. In the night the current works its way over the shoals of your dreams so that when you wake each dawn, you feel like a sojourner at a wayside.

They hung a sign on the highway, printed up brochures, and advertised in bed-and-breakfast guidebooks. As guests started to arrive, Ursula transformed herself from a dirt-under-the-nails earth mover into a demonic housekeeper, a wielder of vacuum cleaners and dust rags. Our boys were banned from all the bathrooms but one, and I'd catch Ursula sneaking in after them even there, vigilant for drops of little-boy pee lingering on the seat.

During the first melt season, the river rose six feet in mid-June. When the wild roses bloomed, an event the Indians say matches the time of highest water, the Yellowstone was hauling along three or four feet below the top of the bank. Muddy green, gritty sounding, the eddy snarling like a whirlpool.

It was impressive enough that when the water went down, Ursula and Dee Dee brought in truckloads of riprap rock, boulders the size of golf carts, and embedded them along the bank to prevent erosion.

The Yellowstone is touted as the last of the free-flowing undammed rivers in the lower forty-eight. Not that it hasn't been targeted. In the mid-1900s the U.S. Army Corps of Engineers and the U.S. Bureau of Reclamation planned dams for every major river in the country and for scores of minor rivers as well. The Yellowstone was plugged on paper like the rest.

The River Inn sits right near to one of the only plausible places to dam the Yellowstone. There the valley narrows down to a rockbound, wind-funneling neck, an obvious spot to cork with concrete. Most of the rest of the river valley is too broad. Only by dint of lucky timing, some layers of porous rock, and strident local opposition was a dam project averted. The fact that the river escaped the fate of the Missouri and Colorado and all the others is not, however, to say that it hasn't been manipulated.

In fact, even to claim that it is undammed is to speak in a narrow sense. Downstream of Billings the Yellowstone is checked in six places by major diversion dams, low-head structures that allow the river to pass but only after diverting irrigation water into canals capable of pulling away, cumulatively, thousands of cubic feet per second.

Beyond that the river is micro managed at every bend.

Farmers drop in pumps to suck up water and build diversion jetties in side channels. Home-owners shore up the bank with rock and steel. People build "barbs" of rock into the current to force it away from their land. They bulldoze berms and levees along the banks. A generation ago, towns along the river used it as a dump. When you float past the town of Big Timber, the steep, high bank is a rusty wall of cans, metal box springs, stoves, and vehicles.

Undammed the Yellowstone may be, in a technical sense, but it's a long way from being free.

During the River Inn's second winter Robert Redford stayed there while he reconnoitered the area for filming his movie, *The Horse Whisperer*. He slept in the Yellow Rock Room, perched above the river. Cakes of sullen-looking ice shifted downstream in the night, rubbing on the shallows like rudderless barges. Dee Dee perfected her German pancake breakfast.

In March it snowed in the mountains almost daily. The snowpack rose well above normal, especially in Yellowstone Park. At Two Ocean Pass, near the Yellowstone's source, water is separated by a divide only a few feet wide. On one side the melt slithers down Atlantic Creek toward Yellowstone Lake and off on a journey to the Gulf of Mexico. On the other side, it descends Pacific Creek into the Snake River and then flows into the Columbia watershed and on to the Pacific. The divide is so narrow that fish have been thought to migrate across it. By the end of March the pass was weighed down under ten-foot blankets of snow.

The cold, wet spring lingered on through April and into May. In the high country snow actually accumulated during May, rather than melting. In early June the rains came, saturating the ground. The Yellowstone jumped three feet overnight after one downpour.

When the hot weather arrived after the first week of June,

the snow started to melt in a terrifying rush. In Yellowstone Park the big lakes climbed to historic highs. Tributary streams spread out of their banks; roads washed out; mudslides blocked highways.

Downstream the Yellowstone turned behemoth. It became a river of mud roiling through the night, rising over islands, taking out chunks of bank in dump-truck-sized gulps. Hot weather settled in and the melt accelerated.

At the River Inn water lapped at the edge of the lawn. The cinder block cellar started to fill up. Ursula installed a sump pump to spew water back into the river. Sandbags were the hot commodity. Friends dropped by to gawk and then joined the work crew building a wall of straw bales and sandbags. In a matter of days they made an island of the house.

The river rose out of its banks and chewed at the highway. Just downstream a row of houses went under to the windowsills. People rafted in and out, rescuing loads of appliances and furniture. To a For Sale sign in front of one flooded house somebody added "Island Property."

Ursula and Dee Dee borrowed horse trailers and emptied the bottom floor. A yearling black bear, as disoriented as the rest of the valley's residents, ran through the yard one morning. At night Ursula and Dee Dee paced the bare rooms, listening to the slick thunder going past and thinking about the weeks they'd lavished on the floors and walls, the money lost, and the relentless, conspiring weather.

Whole mature cottonwood groves came up by the roots and were dragged downstream, turned into leafy battering rams. After several near fatal mishaps involving kayakers with a death wish, authorities closed the watershed to boaters. In a matter of three days a rancher upstream went from having a comfortable buffer 150 feet wide between his house and the river to being able to drop a rock into the current from his porch. The fisheries at several world-renowned spring creeks went under.

In Livingston engineers fretted about the interstate high-way bridge. One of the massive abutments was being erod-ed at an alarming rate where the river rammed into it on a corner. The Yellowstone lapped at the roadbed on the low Ninth Street bridge. The city stationed a backhoe outfitted with huge tongs on the bridge to pluck logs away as they lodged against the pilings.

All but a few residents of Ninth Street Island evacuated. One who remained eschewed sandbags, did nothing to pro-tect his home, and reveled in the show. "Let 'er rip!" he said. His biggest worry was that he'd go to town for supplies and the bridge would wash out so he couldn't get back for the fun.

At the Livingston gauging station the river's flow was measured at more than 32,000 cubic feet per second, the highest rate recorded since the gauge was installed in the early 1900s. Cubic feet per second, or cfs, is one of those hard-to-visualize measurements. Imagine 32,000 one-gallon milk jugs full of river rushing past every second. A milk jug isn't quite a cubic foot, but you get a sense. Flood authori-ties predicted another two-foot rise.

Only the tips of the tallest trees on the island in front of the River Inn still rose out of the water. The current came past at ominous, world-eating speed—dark brown, a mile wide in spots, and carrying a load of sediment so thick it grated like coarse sandpaper. At night the sound seemed to shift and migrate, eerily uncoiling itself, an unruly, untam-able force as irresistible as lava.

Instead of rising, though, the Yellowstone started to drop. An inch at a time, as much as a foot some days, the current fell back past the markers Ursula and Dee Dee had been using as their gauges—the lowest branches of a spruce tree, the sandbag anchoring the outflow pipe from the sump pump. Over several days it slid back down into its banks.

A river is a dynamic, fussy power, forever shifting, nibbling at banks, moving rock, laying down silt, slipping its channel, seeking an elusive equilibrium. A flood only makes blatant what is usually subtle. In ten days the Yellowstone had transformed itself. The island in front of the River Inn migrated thirty yards upstream. The split in the river went from roughly fifty-fifty to more like eighty-twenty, with the channel in front of the bed-and-breakfast shrinking to an anemic flow you'd be hard pressed to get a canoe down.

Everywhere it was the same. Entire islands disappeared; new beaches emerged; twenty-acre hunks of real estate turned to silt and washed downstream; the river's course deepened, widened, and migrated, writhing across the valley. The flood rearranged the furniture, making the terrain seem disorienting and strange to people familiar with the river. Landmarks had disappeared or moved or ceased to be relevant.

Throughout the summer, while mosquitoes rose out of the stagnant leftover floodwater in unprecedented clouds, people rebuilt, moved off, or sold at a loss. The River Inn opened again, largely unscathed. In a moment of dark humor, Dee Dee suggested that they might the name to Inn the River.

Once the looming threat of inundation has receded, the debates rose up. Owners of several of the spring creeks advocated building jetties and levees to mitigate the ravages of future floods. Others insisted that the river be left alone, no matter what the cost to private holdings. At public meetings people shouted at one another. Self-interest pervaded the air like a bad smell. A hydrologist from Denver consulted with local authorities. He suggested building several jetties using cottonwood trees and other natural material to keep the river away from vulnerable sites.

"It comes with the territory," Ursula admitted after one of the meetings. "We bought on a floodplain; we knew that when we made the deal. The river right here is what makes this place beautiful. Being vulnerable to it is the other half of the equation."

The next winter residents watched the snowpack build again. Meteorologists warned that the snowfall was 50 percent greater than the year before throughout much of the state. In February the run on flood insurance began. Even home owners along secondary creeks bought it up.

Through the winter, ice scoured at the river channel. From the bedrooms at the Inn you could hear the slushy mash sliding by and the thud of floes grounding on cobbles. Ice dams built up against bridge abutments and in narrows, backing up the river and then melting open again. In March the noise grew into a constant, growling backdrop. In the rare intervals of quiet, people stopped still, unable to pinpoint their sense of unease, until the next concussion brought it home again. Breakup is a lovely, awesome, thrilling time, but the memory of flood and the oppressive bulk of snow in the peaks turned it ominous and forbidding instead. Dee Dee would start awake in the night, fear in her chest, and lie there listening to the growling river.

Early in the spring Ursula revived her landscaping skills mounding up a two-foot berm set back from the riverbank and planting sod on it. She and Dee Dee extended two barbs of rock from shore, one at the head of the eddy, to push the current farther into the river. Throughout the valley people constructed walls, hoarded sand, and watched the high peaks, pillowed deep with snow. The high school officials in Livingston decided to hold the graduation ceremony on a hillside north of town rather than in the valley. Town authorities announced that they would blow up the Ninth Street bridge if the water came over the top.

A river hydrologist told me that the whole business of 100-year and 500-year floods is a confusing misnomer. Instead there tend to be wet cycles of weather in ten- to twenty-year chunks, so it's actually more likely that there will be back-to-back big floods, or flood years clumped together in a single decade. The concept of 100-year flood events, he said, pans out only in relation to a timeline thousands of years long.

Throughout most of May the melt proceeded at a sedate pace, considering the amount of snow in the hills. The combination of warm days and cool nights swelled the area's rivers to their banks, and kept them there at a steady, barely contained level. Yellowstone Lake broke up weeks ahead of the previous year. People made their sandbag fortifications, covered rows of hay bales with plastic, dug their diversion trenches, and watched the brown flow, thick as a milkshake, hour on hour, day on day.

Until late May only minor flooding marred the outlook. The Shields River, downstream of Livingston, named for one of Lewis and Clark's men and fed by snow in the Crazy Mountains, came out of its banks and into fields and across sections of Highway 89. In other parts of the state there were reports of flooding.

At the end of the month thunderstorms arrived along with high temperatures, the kind of weather you'd normally associate with late August. Over in Big Timber a single storm dropped six inches of rain in two hours. Hail fell with such ferocity that it drifted into knee-high piles. The Boulder River went from containment to full flood in half a day. Flash floods roared down tiny intermittent creeks. The Yellowstone crept out of its banks, spread into cottonwood groves and pastureland, and took out road culverts.

When the wild roses bloomed again at the River Inn, the Yellowstone peaked at more than 37,000 cfs. The sump pump hummed away in the basement. The new berm was the only thing holding the river away from the inn's foundation. The barb in the river, though, proved to be a mixed blessing. At flood stage the eddy it created was a whirlpool fifty feet across. A logjam below the island made an eight-foot wave behind it, a roaring trough of brown. Then the entire jam broke free, floated off, and the river fell smooth.

The workforce materialized again, as did similar crews all over the valley. Actors from Robert Redford's movie heaved sandbags with the rest. Ursula and Dee Dee worked until dark and then retreated inside to listen through the black hours to the thick torrent humping past, five paces from the back door. Every two hours they got up, like ranchers during calving season, to make their rounds of the property boundaries, to listen for the sump pump, and to check the low spots in the fortifications. A parade of cottonwood trees, clumps of alders, pieces of front porch, firewood, foundered boats, and lawn furniture slid past. Each morning they checked their gauges, took the river's pulse, called up the weather on the computer screen, and got the current cfs reading from the Internet.

For almost two weeks the Yellowstone held at two feet above flood stage. Rock and forest started to appear on the high mountain peaks. The snowpack dwindled away, feeding the flood. The River Inn held its own, a topographic island with one foot of freeboard. If the river broke through one bend upstream or if it backed up downstream, the house would go under. Once they finished their own sandbag walls, they worked for two days at the upstream neighbor's.

Ursula and Dee Dee lost weight. They acquired that haggard, wiry, half-crazed elated look universal to disaster victims. The river was a force they'd hitched themselves to, in an intimate relationship with a partner magnificent, terrifying, joyous, insidious, and impartial as an avalanche.

When the flood crest moved downstream in mid-June, a bulge of water rippling across 600 miles of Montana, it left the River Inn undamaged again. The sump pump thumped away for another week and then stopped.

In mid-July I went over to visit. At first glance everything looked normal, but then the alterations started to sink in, as if someone had come in and airbrushed changes in a photograph I thought I knew. The river was six feet below its bank, but it was still silty green, still strong enough to make me think twice about putting a boat into it.

River sand coated the lawn in a thin beach deposit. The spruce tree hung precariously over the bank, roots exposed. Because of the barbs the river corner had shifted slightly upstream. Below the lower barb a new beach had been laid in. The island had become two islands, with a shallow chute of water chattering through the middle. Again, it had moved noticeably upstream. There were new lobes of gravel bar, a fresh shape to realign with. The river had regained some of its flow in the near channel. Across the way the view seemed more open and uncluttered.

"They lost thirty feet of land and a whole grove of cottonwoods over there," Ursula said.

Plans for improving the flood barricades were already under way: putting more rock in the river bank, extending the berm and heightening it here and there, putting in some soil-anchoring vegetation. The way she talked, I could tell that Ursula had been busy mapping fortifications in her mind for months.

We decided to take the canoe across to the island. Sawyer came, too, wearing an oversized life vest. I tied him to me with half-inch rope.

"We don't have to do this," Ursula said before we got in,

and I almost backed off. Two years running the Yellowstone had unveiled its power. To be on it again was like being in the company of an old friend after a bout of madness.

It was a strangely tense crossing—the eddy a tricky vortex, green upwellings alongshore, a disquieting murkiness to the water. Over on the island the gravel was all new, immigrant rock uprooted from other lands. Sawyer found a cow's rib. There were hunks of green quartzite and a few agates—all fresh looking, just washed, blinking in the sun.

"This river is such a living force," Ursula said. "It could all change again tomorrow."

Taking the Yellowstone by Storm

Every trip has its moment of truth. This one had several. First, before the boat is even baptized in the flow, at the sandbar put-in just upriver from the bridge near Reedpoint, we are faced with a daunting pile of gear to fit in our red, seventeen-foot canoe. Family tent, sleeping bags, life jackets, food for two weeks, sacks of diapers, miniature folding chairs, rubber ducks, water jugs—it all spills, piece by piece, from the open maw of our vehicle.

Eli, Sawyer, and Ruby, all aged four or younger, busy themselves throwing rocks, eating sand, and wandering off into the shrubbery. All of this—the food and gear, five human beings, the toys and buckets, everything—is to fit inside the sleek hull of the canoe. More than that, once ensconced, we are to move downriver for a couple of weeks, borne along on the burgeoning current of the Yellowstone within months of a hundred-year flood.

Loading the canoe takes us the better part of an hour. Several items deemed essential a short while earlier are returned to the vehicle. Every crevice in the canoe is stuffed with gear. The children, life vests riding up under their chins, sun hats squashed in place, and full of good questions like "Do you think we'll sink, Dad?" are wedged into their spots between duffels and water jugs.

The Yellowstone is a habit-forming river. For fifteen years I've repeated favorite stretches—the whitewater intensity through Yankee Jim Canyon, mountain-rimmed pieces of Paradise Valley, the weekend meander from Springdale to Reedpoint. In 1992, back when Eli was an infant, our compact family rode down the entire navigable length, from Yellowstone Park to North Dakota, on a twenty-five-day jaunt.

I've even been enticed out of hibernation by freak February thaws to put in at Emigrant and paddle to Livingston, and it isn't every river that can accomplish that. The Yellowstone is more than a watercourse; it is another one of the vices I seem so prone to. My abiding hope is that my children will succumb to the same addiction.

This journey is necessarily open-ended. Flexibility is one of the requirements of parenthood. On a family boat trip, it may be the key ingredient to remaining sane. The starting point is a fishing access roughly a day's float upstream of Columbus and about a third of the way along the river. We have two or three weeks available. The take-out is intentionally uncertain. A friend has agreed to deliver our vehicle, on short notice, to whatever spot we select downstream. Along with every nonessential item in our outfit, we have jettisoned the pressure of deadlines and destinations in favor of a wherever-we-get-to paddling regime.

Despite five passengers and our bulging outfit, the canoe does float. Ruby, our mobile, energetic, and headstrong one-year-old, demands the constant vigilance of the bow paddler. She is tethered by rope to whichever parent is in the front, an umbilical cord in case of capsize. The boys are seated in low-slung director's chairs, obscured from the shoulders down in the mass of gear. My perspective from the cramped stern seat takes in the sobering overview of the gypsy craft Marypat and I are responsible for.

I remind myself that we could be home, busy juggling the chores in a day and keeping a lid on the frenetic energy now constrained by the hull of our canoe. In short order the Yellowstone begins to unfold its spell. Great blue herons lift off the banks. An osprey hovers, tense and focused, above an eddy. At a sharp bend where the river runs hard into a ledge of sandstone, a mule deer clatters heavily up the near vertical slope. Where the river eddies in the cool shadow of an undercut cliff, we coast beneath the mud-daubed nests of swallows and catch drips seeping from rock seams.

We come to shore often to indulge exploratory impulses. The kids find a sun-warmed pool full of tadpoles and plunge in to terrorize the inhabitants. Eli and Sawyer quickly become expert at scaling rough-barked cottonwood trunks in piles of flood debris. At lunch stops we wade into the cold, translucent flow. The river, pressing downhill, is forceful and muscular. It piles around us, beginning the relentless job of erosion against the pillars of our legs. I hold the boys by their arms and the river pulls them out flat so they are surfing across the top.

Between Reedpoint and Billings the water is frequently challenging. The steady current is punctuated by abrupt drops down ramps of cobbles, tricky chutes with three-foot waves at the bottom, and eddies strong enough to dunk us all if we don't brace for them. There are ninety-degree corners where the river does its damnedest to pull our canoe up against the ledgy shore. We try to skirt the sets of large standing waves that crop up every few miles. They would be great fun if we were paddling alone, but a boat full of sloshing water and wet children is pretty far down on the list of our desires.

Near Park City we encounter a piece of fast water with big waves that we can't avoid. Right at the start Eli tosses out a rubber duck that he thinks is tied to the thwart but which, to his horror, has come unmoored. It goes bobbing downstream to the tune of his keening. Just then we dive over the first wave and take on a slug of river that douses Ruby to her armpits. More water slops over the side, wetting the boys. Eli is still mourning the lost duck, and now Sawyer responds loudly to the unexpected shock of cold river.

"Get to shore!" Marypat yells.

"Everybody shut up!" I counter.

There is a second set of waves before we can make for the safety of the near bank, more water in the canoe, and a rising crescendo of children crying and high-decibel spousal interaction.

The summer flood has rearranged the Yellowstone, providing a fresh set of surprises. There are new channels cut through some islands, and other islands have washed away completely; rafts of trees have come downriver to settle on gravel bars; chunks of bank have sloughed off. Some entire trees, green leaves fluttering in the current, are dangerously aground in the middle of the flow.

In a ten-mile stretch upstream and downstream of Laurel, the river spreads through a series of shallows where floodborne trees litter the watercourse. Time after time we slide around a bend on the cantering flow and find trees jamming half the river's width or hanging up in the precise spot where the Yellowstone most wants to push us. We pick channels between gravel bars with the ominous feeling of playing watery roulette. The children pick up on our tension and sit quietly. Even Ruby gets the message. Paddling alone, the obstacles would be unremarkable. With children aboard, the strain makes me struggle for air, in the same way driving on icy roads with a carload of kids makes me sweat.

For the first week the sky is blue and the days hot. We slide through Columbus and under the new bridge construction at Laurel. Besides an occasional drift boat and one or two motorboats, there is no one else on the river. The tent goes up on a shady island below Columbus, on cobbly shoreline at the outskirts of Billings, and along a quiet, unmarred side channel where I wouldn't be surprised by a herd of buffalo at sunset or the silhouette of a Crow rider on the bluff.

Across from the power plant in Billings and upstream from the interstate bridge, our canoe coasts through the shadow of Sacrifice Cliffs. When natives of the Northwest were being decimated by the smallpox plague during the 1830s—legacy of fur trapper, explorer, cavalry scout, and early settler—some threw themselves off the high yellow escarpment and into the river in an attempt to appease the Great Spirit.

Our daily mileage varies with the mood in the boat—as few as ten miles when the kids are fussy and bored, as many as twenty-five when Ruby naps and the boys entertain each other by creating wildlife dioramas on the packs with their plastic animals. The children are all at high-maintenance ages. Much as they'd like to pitch in, the fact is that Marypat and I stuff every sleeping bag, tie every shoe, clean every dish, load every pack, cook every meal, paddle every stroke, and put toothpaste on every toothbrush.

In theory, after we put the kids down at dusk, the two of us could return to the fire for a quiet interlude of stargazing, with the river whispering past: camp life the way it used to be. In fact, it's all I can do most evenings to outlast the kids long enough to jot a few notes in my journal. Often as not I am asleep before they are.

Truth is, there are moments when we wonder if it is worth it, but then we coast past a flock of white pelicans and Ruby is holding herself up by the gunwale, literally dancing with excitement. Then I see the two boys, barely three feet tall, running across their sandbar kingdom in the waning light. Not one of them is five years into life, but they don't bat an eye at sleeping outside, sitting on rocks to eat their dinner, or listening to a great horned owl hooting above the tent.

Conscious memories they may not keep, but a marrow-deep knowledge—of a river on the move, summer winds, sand under bare feet, yellow cliffs rising sheer out of the water—will lodge somewhere as primordial and formative as their first sensory grappling with the universe.

Two days downstream of Billings we climb to the top of Pompey's Pillar. In 1806, William Clark stopped here long enough to etch his name in the soft sandstone and immortalize the squat pillar in honor of Sacajawea's son. He and his contingent were traveling fast for St. Louis, paddling a crude catamaran of two lashed-together twenty-eight-foot dugout cottonwood trees as many as eighty miles in a day.

The sandstone landmark also stands as a kind of gateway to the land of Indian wars. From the top, looking across the river and up a broad valley bordered by low, dry hills, it doesn't require much of a leap to imagine the ranks of cavalry horses, and the creaking artillery carts, the supply wagons that camped there two generations after Clark mapped the valley. The Yellowstone may have the singular distinction of being the river most heavily adorned with town sites named after military men of that era: Custer, Terry, Miles City, Forsyth.

Between Pompey's Pillar and the mouth of the Bighorn River we camp along a stretch of fast water where Marypat and I take giddy turns swimming, with our life vests on, through the waves and riffles. The boys hang on to our shoulders while we whirl ponderously in a broad eddy. It is both a fun ride and an important lesson in the curriculum of river knowledge. Eddy Currents 101.

There, for the first time, we start finding chunks of river-weathered petrified wood and moss agate in the gravel. Eli and Sawyer are transformed from tree climbers and sand excavators into rock hounds with respectably keen eyes. By morning the canoe weight we'd lost by consuming ten days' worth of food is more than replaced by their bucketful of "keepers."

The river, now, has a more sedate feel to it. We coast along for miles under circling red-tailed hawks, letting the current do the work. Occasional diversion dams, some with warning signs and others without, are the most pressing danger. The land has, more and more, the feel of eastern Montana—pastel badland colors, short-grass prairie, arid buttes, and horizons of quiet.

In 1807, when St. Louis marked the western edge of the American frontier, Manuel Lisa built the first of a succession of fur-trading posts near the Yellowstone's confluence with the Bighorn River. His was the first stab of exploitation and settlement along the river. He ushered in the era of trappers, steamboat commerce, military campaigns, and the early waves of permanent settlers. Well downstream, near Sidney, an old railroad bridge across the Yellowstone is still outfitted with the drawbridge section that steamboats passed under.

Almost two weeks out the next moment of truth strikes our expedition. As usual, camp is on an exposed bar below the high-water mark. There are billowy thunderheads and distant lightning in the west when we retire.

Sometime later, the night as black as the inside of a box, the storm pounces. Marypat and I jerk awake to a wind that is collapsing one side of the tent. Rain hammers down, loud as hail. Half naked, we brace ourselves against the windward wall, holding up the taut, straining nylon and bent poles. My face is pressed to the mosquito-netting window. Outside, the night alternates between purple blackness and stabs of searing brilliance. Lightning stitches across whole quadrants of the western horizon, forks with hot vengeance to the ground, and fills the clouds with its monstrous wattage. In the moments of illumination I see the canoe turned over onshore, our stash of gear wrapped in a tarp, the ghostly trunks of cottonwood, and the dim outline of cliffs across the river.

Eli wakes up, whimpering. Ruby starts to wail. Between gusts of wind that feel like body punches we comfort them, telling them it's just a rainstorm. Sawyer slumbers through the whole thing. His sleeping bag is the dam soaking up a stream of water pouring into the tent and the wall above him is collapsing on his face, but he never wakes.

By morning the tent is a sodden, sandy mess, all the sleeping bags are wet, and we emerge into the mist like earthquake survivors climbing out of the rubble. Fortunately, the day clears and warms up. Dry clothes and several rounds of hot chocolate restore a measure of cheerfulness. By mid-morning the sleeping bags are dry enough to pack away. A couple of hours' worth of bright sun reduces the trauma of the storm to a good story. Our only worry is that Marypat is battling a mysterious foot infection that seems to be getting worse rather than better.

Two days later it happens again. Summer warmth is swept away by an abrupt cold front—scudding clouds, a cold upriver wind, plummeting temperatures. In the course of an hour we go from shorts and T-shirts to coats and wool caps.

This time we are smart enough to locate camp in a sheltered thicket, but the storm is, if anything, worse than the first. Rain is a constant, drumming sheet, hour after hour. Eventually the tent succumbs. Trickles invade, then streams and pools. All the bags are damp, and several get soaked through. One of the kids wets the bed for good measure.

Dawn is not cheering, only more of the same dismal stuff cast in gray light.

Marypat's foot is painful and swollen enough now that she walks only with difficulty. When the rain eases off to a steady drizzle, we assess our position. The small town of Hysham is a mile or two away. If we don't stop now the next reasonable access will be several days' travel downstream, at Forsyth.

In light of Marypat's condition, not to mention the scene in the tent, the decision isn't much of an intellectual challenge. Suddenly this point along the riverbank seems as good a place as any to negotiate the end of our journey and call for our car. Within an hour I have camp battened down and everyone in rain gear. We begin what becomes known as The Hobble to Hysham, down a rain-slick farm road full of promises of pancakes, bacon, and cocoa at the café we fervently hope will be waiting.

Behind us the Yellowstone rolls on through the drizzle toward the Missouri. I play a game with the kids, walking backward and looking across the valley so that the next time we turn around, the grain elevator in town will seem closer. What I don't tell them is that I am also indulging in my own final embrace with the river.

Wind

EVEN AT DAWN there is a restlessness in the air, an uneasiness. Smoke from the fire and wafts of the aroma of brewing coffee strike me in the face. The air is stirring ahead of time, I think, but no one else seems to notice the early breezes.

Our two canoes lie on the mud bank of the White River, near the border between Colorado and Utah. On this trip adults are outnumbered by children. We have three in our boat, and Andrew and Sara have two in theirs. We have become more prone to inviting friends along on our outings than we were in our more solitary and ambitious paddling era. Our kids like the company of other families, the adults can share in child care, and there is a measure of safety if things go wrong. Marypat's brother, Andrew, has managed a week's leave of absence from teaching and has driven down with Sara and their two kids to join us.

Our winter expedition planning energy is also informed by a different set of parameters from those we followed before we had kids. We look for family-friendly water—rivers with minor rapids, a lack of portages, country with the potential for fun excursions. The White has all this, but it is a small, seasonal river with a brief spring window of adequate flow.

It is early in the season, just the end of April. In the high desert the weather vacillates between warm and balmy and chilly enough to be uncomfortable. On some days we wear shorts and T-shirts; on others we layer on coats and hats. If our feet get wet when we are launching the boats, they might stay numb half the morning.

The water is mud gray, high with snowmelt, clicking along. This is oil and gas country, arid, rocky land webbed with dirt roads, storage tanks, rusty pipelines, and pumps rocking like metronomes. The White, like most rivers, asserts a measure of remove from the country it flows through. It remains aloof from the activity that hovers nearby, eluding it by virtue of its erratic, tricky pulse, its dramatic topography, and its abiding proclivity for erosion. An occasional power line crosses its path; one or two dirt tracks follow its banks; we see a pipeline on a dayhike.

For the most part the river is its own ribboning world. On it we slip the grasp of civilization and are alone. There are broken weathered cliffs looming over the corners, sandstone abraded into goblin shapes, cottonwood groves and beavers, eagles on updrafts. A day upstream three small, shaggy wild horses watched us paddle up close with that wary, outlaw glint in their eyes.

After breakfast Marypat and Sara suggest a hike before we take to the canoes. We straggle off toward the rising sun over parched land, sand washes, badland gullies, and moon rock. Lizards do push-ups in patches of sunlight. I listen for rattlers in the sagebrush. We take portraits of the five cousins in caves of sandstone. All the while I notice the winds picking up, flapping the hoods of our jackets and raising little tornado spouts of dust.

By the time we return and pack up, the wind is a force we lean our weight against, an invisible wall coming up the valley. It bullies us on the trail down to the boats, slaps the kids around, and roughs up the river. The strongest gusts rush across the water like fast trains, loud and arresting. We see them sandpapering toward us, lifting spray.

It takes Andrew and Sara three tries to get out of the eddy below camp. Between the current curling back and the wind punching at the bow, they go in circles for minutes. Marypat and I are far more experienced, but it is all we can do to go straight downstream. The kids push their hands down between their thighs for warmth and hunker behind packs with their wool hats pulled over their ears.

When a big gust comes at us broadside, we brace with our paddles in the water and hang on while the boat skips across the current. The canoes bang against the banks, scrape into overhanging branches, and get captured by eddies. I can see that Andrew and Sara are engaged in strident conversation, their faces wrought up with the struggle, but can hear nothing over the buffeting air. On one sandy corner both of the boats are slammed onto a gravel bar. We literally cannot turn around. Finally, in a short lull, we skitter backward into the next straightaway.

In the rare windows of calm the sun feels warm, the current regains its steady momentum, and I think what a good day for paddling it might be.

Wind is one of the invisible gods, like gravity or like love. It is with us always, intangible and elusive but inescapable. It is the breathing of the earth. It has no color, no taste, and no smell, but it can rip roofs off buildings, whipsaw bridges, uproot trees, founder ships . . . and pin us down when everything else in a day is right for paddling on.

We have fretted away five days on a tundra lake waiting for the wind to die and the waves to calm. Five days and five nights without a break. People we know have given up trips altogether because the wind wouldn't allow them passage. On some water we have gotten up to paddle at three in the morning for six days running to escape the gales, and more than once in a boat we have taken chances with wind and felt our lives swinging in the airy balance. The capsize on Opacopa Lake early in my paddling career is a memory seared indelibly onto some subconscious layer. That desperate, windy afternoon snaps back sharp and breathtaking every time a wind springs its ambush.

Our planet's atmosphere wraps it in a quilt that weighs 5,600 million million tons. More than three-quarters of that weight is settled just overhead, in a layer only ten miles thick called the troposphere, where weather happens.

If the earth's topography, heat distribution, and surface color were uniform, the atmosphere would lie on us like a quiet cocoon, an unimaginable stillness. But the planet is wrinkled with mountain ranges and broken into a patchwork of blue oceans and green forests and white polar regions. The sun shines on us directly or obliquely, depending on the time of year and our location.

More than anything it is the heat of the sun, and the contrast between warm and cool masses of air, that stirs the atmospheric soup. On a global scale air moves in great convection cells that span twenty degrees of latitude, heating and rising at the equator, for instance, creating a vacuum into which more air rushes from north and south. As the equatorial air rises, it cools and grows dense, is pushed north or south, and finally falls back down in vast mountains of high pressure.

It's more complicated and subtle than that, of course. There are high-altitude rivers, jet streams, that rush along the margins of warm and cool air masses at speeds of more than 500 miles per hour. The spinning of the earth bends the air as it flows, creating prevailing winds and dominant weather patterns by virtue of the Coriolis effect.

Local conditions and topography complicate wind patterns as well. Bare mountain peaks tend to heat up quickly during the day, drawing winds up slope, toward the warmth. At night the forested valleys trap heat longer and the winds flip around, moving downslope. Onshore and offshore breezes along coasts are the result of the unequal heating of beaches and water.

Some regions have such notable local winds that they've earned distinctive names: The chinooks of the Rocky Mountains. Williwaws in Australia. The bora. Sirocco. Datoo. Winds that suck up a foot of snow in an hour, build ocean waves fifty feet high, and lather up sandstorms that render day into night.

Winds carry an astonishing load of freight. Even in the purest polar air, there are a quarter of a million microscopic bits of foreign material in every lungful. At rush hour in a major city, every breath we take is loaded with 375 million particles. Plant seeds, bacteria, tiny insects, spores of fungi, tons of topsoil—all of it moving, sometimes for thousands of miles, on the snaking rivers of air. Tiny insects called springtails are regularly deposited in snowy Arctic regions and then live there quite comfortably on the bits of forage brought to them by the windy catering service. During the dust bowl era, ships anchored in New York Harbor were coated with topsoil from Oklahoma.

There is evidence that humans are not immune to the effects of wind, either, and that we respond physiologically to the exhalations of the atmosphere. Our pace quickens; we lean forward into a confrontational posture. Our pupils expand, a sign of heightened awareness. Blood vessels constrict or dilate to adjust body temperature. Our metabolic rate picks up. The heart beats faster.

On the White River the wind is funneling up the valley in waves that feel like physical blows and our hearts are beating fast. We are working hard, for one thing, and we have no business being out here, for another. Within a mile I am looking for a place to stop.

Andrew and Sara careen from one bank to the other, faces grim and strained. Their kids clutch at the canoe gunwales. Marypat and I ram up on a sandbank to discuss our options, but we have waited one bend too long.

We watch them struggle down toward the corner. A gust shoves them halfway across the river and pins them against a submerged log. The canoe starts to tip, but they manage to right themselves. Andrew is flailing with his paddle, trying to balance between the wind clutching at the hull and the grasp of current holding them fast to the log. Slowly they slide their way down the trunk and get free, only to sail broadside into a clump of roots on the corner of the bend.

We are out of our boat, standing helplessly on the far shore. I see branches whip the kid's faces. Sara and Andrew are yelling something I can't make out, hauling desperately through the clump of roots. The boat broaches and nearly capsizes; water sloshes in. Somehow they work free.

"Get to shore!" I scream. "Land anywhere you can."

They end up fifty yards downstream, on a sloping rock at the base of a sheer dirt bank five feet high. We paddle across, clawing through the wind, and manage to slide our boat up on the same rock. No one brings up the possibility of finding a better landing site. We hug each other on the brink of the river.

"Let's get lunch out and see what happens," Marypat says. "Maybe it will calm down later."

Like deer yarding up in winter we push through dense

shrubbery into a small, protected clearing surrounded by thorny shrubs. It is warm here, and calm. Our faces relax. But in the cottonwoods overhead wind streams through the leaves like a strong tide ripping through eelgrass. The willows alongshore double over in supplication. The noise is a thing we have to raise our voices against.

Every so often I go to check the boats. They are hauled up barely out of the river on the rock, tied off to clumps of sage.

I pull out the maps, as I have, I think, in every place I have ever been windbound. If we can't travel today, we are twenty miles short of the itinerary. If it is windy again tomorrow, our trip plans are sunk. There is a dirt road that comes within a mile of the opposite bank. It leads to a paved road three miles away, which goes to an oil town. That is our escape route if the worst happens and we are pinned down for good, I decide. It is not an outcome I have the least interest in.

My calculations are only the latest in a twenty-year string of shore-fast figurings along pieces of water that span the continent. How much food do we have? What happens if we are a day late? Two days? If we make no progress today, how many miles will we have to average to catch up again? What is the landscape like ahead? Is there another escape route downriver? Sometimes I conclude that the wind is a welcome and pleasant excuse for a layover day, a Sunday on the trail. More often I feel as if I am trying to make a paycheck span a month's expenses and discovering that it will just make it, providing I don't eat.

"Let's go for a hike," Sara suggests. "The map shows a tributary canyon just around the corner."

The tributary is dry. It ascends a series of steps and ledges never quite high enough to stop us, to a plateau of barren rock and frail soil fine as chalk. The kids scramble after lizards along the scaly rock faces. We walk to a low pass between valleys, a saddle where the wind rips off my hat and blows it fifty feet downslope. We can barely stand there in the blast. On the overhanging spine of a sharp hogback ridge I can look directly down at the river. The red stern of one of the canoes pokes out from under the bank three hundred feet down. I could jump for it.

The day wanes. We return to the boats and decide to unpack dinner but hold off on the tents; there might still be an evening lull. There isn't. In the cold, gray twilight the gusts are undiminished. We eat chili with gloves on, behind a windscreen of shrubs.

"What's the plan?" Andrew asks.

"We get up at first light and hope it's calm," I say. "If it is, we have miles to make up. If it isn't, we might start thinking of plan B, whatever that is."

It is my turn to share a tent with Ruby; Marypat is in the other small tent with Eli and Sawyer. The bedtime ritual with Ruby these days involves singing several rounds of "Rudolph the Red-Nosed Reindeer," followed by "How Much Is That Doggie in the Window?" until the eyelids start to sag. Ruby is not yet two. I realize that this is her first wind-bound experience.

Finally she breathes her deep infant breaths next to me, but I lie awake listening to the wind rushing through the darkness. I think about the dead cottonwood branches creaking overhead and the way Andrew and Sara looked, how pale and desperate their faces were, in the dirty roots of the snag just upstream.

Wind is one of those Zen tests, one that I have faced dozens of times and that I usually fail. It involves humility and patience and an acceptance of the unknowable, things I am not particularly gifted at. Once, though, months into a very long trip, I spent an entire windbound afternoon sitting on a lakeside shelf of quartzite, doing absolutely nothing. I didn't eat. I didn't write or read. I hardly moved. The waves crashed in. The clouds scurried past. The sun made its arc. I don't even remember what I thought, except, late in the day, to recognize that I had managed something graceful and deep.

Disappearing Acts

 I N DAWN LIGHT that is as much
night as day, we gather at the fire with Andrew and Sara. The
kids are still asleep, and we use the time to cook up some
oatmeal and start to pack. It is cold but absolutely still along
the White River. The wind has granted us a release, a small
blessing, another in the string that stretches back half my life
and beyond. Blessings and miracles. Marypat's first pregnancy taking hold in the tiny northern cabin; Craig and
Susan's revival from the clutches of hypothermia; a provi-
dential cow track along a dusty Montana trail; a season of
remarkable connections with birds; the welcome of pod after
pod of beluga whales. More of it coming all the time, like
spring runoff.

Every one a gift of water, itself miraculous and unfathomable.

The first time I watched a water miracle unfold, I was a
month out of college, back at the beginning of all this. There
were five of us, school friends, one a professor with two
young daughters. We had driven from Indiana to hike in the

Wyoming mountains, had been rebuffed there by deep snows lingering in the high peaks, and had ended up in northern New Mexico, at Bandelier National Monument.

It was my first desert immersion. We left the Ford LTD parked in the shade of a ponderosa pine grove, laden with jettisoned mountaineering gear—wool pants, stiff leather boots, ice axes. We stripped down and walked into the aridity.

Everything was first-time new, exotic, and sharply defined: the gritty volcanic tuff full of swallow's nests and cliff dwellings, the latticework stalks of walking-stick cholla, the vanilla smell of ponderosa bark.

Things leapt at me, eager to be discovered. In one camp there was a hummingbird nest the size of a dollhouse teacup in the chest-high, forking branch of a cottonwood, with two white eggs smaller than navy beans inside. On the ground at a ruin I picked up a tiny, perfect obsidian arrowhead, still sharp enough to pierce hide, flaked so thin the sun shone through the smoky lens.

Deep in the backcountry, on a day hike, we bushwhacked up a series of dry washes, tapping ahead with cholla canes to alert rattlers. The rock was burnt basalt, full of tiny holes. Two wild burros clattered across a hillside. We followed their trail over desiccated, spiny ground and through a low pass between drainages. Around a corner the basalt dropped away sheer. A narrow ledge led a few feet into space and then tapered to nothing.

Above the ledge, covering a rock panel the size of a large painter's canvas, were designs pecked in the sun-hot rock. Antlered animals, blocky human figures, snakes or lightning bolts, a sun—all etched, a dot at a time, into the hardened volcanic flow. Taking turns, we edged out over the chasm, feeling the sun on our necks. Heat pulsed off the rock in waves. We each imagined ourselves alone, stripped to loincloth and moccasin, tapping out the patterns that tied us in some inextricable way to our grasp of the world. Then we each sidled back, without a word, our faces seared with rock heat.

Above one of our camps, on Capulin Creek, overlooking the small valley and carved into layers of volcanic ash and lava, sat Painted Cave. White-throated swifts scythed through the hot air in front of it. This was a place of veneration and ritual for the ancients who lived in the high tributary canyons off the Rio Grande—a shallow navel in soft rock decorated with angular, faded art and ocher handprints, hanging there through the centuries.

A desert place. Dust gray mourning doves dozed in the creosote and acacia, their dry calls silenced. The afternoon air was still, shimmering above the ground, buzzing faintly with some undefinable energy made of insect wings and opening acacia pods and the rotating earth.

Capulin Creek was a small, clear, out-of-place flow descending from somewhere cooler and forested, where snow rests in shadows through the winter and springs seep from hillsides. Late in the day we waded in, ankle-deep, as if, like plants, to take refreshment by capillary action up the stalks of our legs. The shallow water broke smoothly around us like filaments of silk, a liquid seduction that, once we entered, we couldn't leave.

We played there. Soon we started building small dams, setting flat stones into walls, creating pools to our knees. The girls lay down in the water. Coolness ran through us. The creek noise blocked out the sun and dust as the clear current felt its way through the rocky bed and downhill toward the murky green fatness of the Rio Grande.

Then, as if in response to the slow turning of a tap, Capulin Creek diminished. At first it was only an impression, a vague lessening of pressure against the ankles. But then a lip of damp sand appeared along the bank, the walls of our dams rose up and dried in the sun, and the pools went stagnant and filtered slowly away. It felt strangely personal, as if we were guilty of a monstrous indiscretion—entering the water, making light of it, manipulating it—and were responsible for it deserting this ceremonial place.

We retreated to the warm shade and watched the water disappear. By the time we finished dinner, Capulin Creek was gone. But for one or two small pools, some wet sand, and a whiff of cool air, it might never have been there at all.

Night came on, quiet and black. We talked softly, listening for something, remembering the chuckle of water. We slept through the stillness in our cocoons of down under Painted Cave. At first light the air was clear as water, washed and pale. The doves cooed to one another in their timeless way, a desert call to prayer at dawn.

Capulin Creek had returned. I could hear it from under the tarp and slid out of the sleeping bag's warmth to go and hunker next to it, holding my knees hard against my chest in the gray morning.

THE WAY water keeps coming and coming, renewing itself, is the obvious miracle. But how it can disappear in an afternoon and be back again in the morning is the one I never have figured out. Almost a quarter of a century later, it happened again.

The springs that feed this ephemeral fork of White Beaver Creek in central Montana lie only a mile or two up the canyon. There, along some seam of impermeability—a clay or shale leaf laid into the dominant pages of sandstone— water oozes out in the shade of ponderosa pines, dampens the earth, and nourishes lush grasses in a landscape other-wise notable for vegetation good at going thirsty. Prickly pears, junipers, sage—plants with roots that are hungry, weathered tendrils reaching across open rock in a slow grope for moist openings.

Springwater weeps down the hillsides and funnels into low spots, seeking company, until it coalesces in the sharply defined little canyon that has broken through the sandstone bench and rendered a slice of the sparse, dusty country grudgingly, and sporadically, riparian.

When the water flows, it is a magnet. Mule deer nuzzle into the water then, porcupine and wild turkeys and coyotes come. There are frogs along the banks, water striders skating in the pools, and mosquitoes in the air. Yellow-rumped warblers and pine siskins and nighthawks forage through the airborne pantry of insect pickings. Bats flutter at twilight like canvas-winged butterflies. A Cooper's hawk tilts through the underbrush, a predatory shadow driving sparrows and warblers into the thickets.

All night the stream sings through the rocks, picking at the sandstone, giving teat to the thick-barked cottonwoods, to the ponderosa pines with roots fat as anacondas, to the skittish creatures that the great horned owl seeks with moon-colored eyes from its perch in an overhanging snag.

When the water flows, we come too, drawn by the same gravitational force that pulls the springwater. Off the sandstone bluffs where we own a patch of land, down along the narrow game trails, and through the warm summer shade where red-breasted nuthatches scrabble in the tree bark and prickly pears wait in ambush for the unwary foot.

The kids strip naked and wade in like amphibians that have gone dry too long. They race pine cones or sticks or rubber ducks, find waterfalls and thigh-deep holes and inch-long frogs. For a time the rocks in the stream course are the territory of garish plastic dinosaurs.

The children lie on their naked bellies and plunge their

faces in to drink from the stream. I'll be damned if I'm going to deny them that feral pleasure, to intrude with some weird filter or drop of bleach. Let them drink. I'll drink, too. If things have come to the point that we can't take water within two miles of a spring-fed source, I want to know about it.

Sometime in July the water fades. The flow that in April and May was milky with sandstone grit, full of the detritus of pine forest, and cold as snowmelt, has become clear as glass, a quiet energy that seeks the least arduous way, that lingers in warm pools as if savoring passage, a channel so narrow that a two-year-old can step across.

Then we like to pitch our tent and camp next to it, where we can palpate the failing yearly pulse. Near the end the water dries up each day, waning against the July heat and the demands of roots and porous stone. At night, then, the stream is a string of pools waiting for the thread of current. At dawn, for a time, it is back. We have our coffee next to it. The birds come. It is cool as a church.

But a week later it is finally gone. The stones are dusty. There are grasshoppers along the banks. The waterfalls are lips of dry rock the boys jump from, wary of sunning rattlesnakes. The deer go elsewhere to drink or go without. We keep coming back, periodically, expectant in spite of ourselves, and cast about for the last shaded pool, a final persistent spring, some sign to reassure memory and insist on hope.